Stolen Years

Stolen Years

A Memoir of Simranjit Singh Mann's Imprisonment

PAVIT KAUR

PENGUIN
VIKING
An imprint of Penguin Random House

VIKING

USA | Canada | UK | Ireland | Australia
New Zealand | India | South Africa | China | Singapore

Viking is part of the Penguin Random House group of companies whose addresses can be found at global.penguinrandomhouse.com

Published by Penguin Random House India Pvt. Ltd
4th Floor, Capital Tower 1, MG Road,
Gurugram 122 002, Haryana, India

Penguin Random House India

First published in Vintage by Random House India 2014
Published in Viking by Penguin Random House India 2018

All photographs by courtesy of the author.

10 9 8 7 6 5 4 3 2

ISBN 9788184004427

Typeset in Linux Libertine by R. Ajith Kumar
Printed at Replika Press Pvt. Ltd, India

www.penguin.co.in

FSC www.fsc.org MIX Paper from responsible sources FSC® C016779

For my father and all the other men and women who have suffered at the hands of a State's atrocities.

And for my mother, a very brave lady . . .

If–

If you can keep your head when all about you
    Are losing theirs and blaming it on you,
If you can trust yourself when all men doubt you,
    But make allowance for their doubting too;
If you can wait and not be tired by waiting,
    Or being lied about, don't deal in lies,
Or being hated, don't give way to hating,
    And yet don't look too good, nor talk too wise:

If you can dream–and not make dreams your master;
    If you can think–and not make thoughts your aim;
If you can meet with Triumph and Disaster
    And treat those two imposters just the same;
If you can bear to hear the truth you've spoken
    Twisted by knaves to make a trap for fools,
Or watch the things you gave your life to, broken,
    And stoop and build 'em up with worn-out tools:

If you can make one heap of all your winnings
    And risk it on one turn of pitch-and-toss,
And lose, and start again at your beginnings
    And never breathe a word about your loss;
If you can force your heart and nerve and sinew
    To serve your turn long after they are gone,

And so hold on when there is nothing in you
    Except the Will which says to them: 'Hold on!'
If you can talk with crowds and keep your virtue,
    Or walk with Kings—nor lose the common touch,
If neither foes nor loving friends can hurt you,
    If all men count with you, but none too much;
If you can fill the unforgiving minute
    With sixty seconds' worth the distance run,
Yours is the Earth and everything that's in it,
    And—which is more—you'll be a Man, my son!

—Rudyard Kipling

PROLOGUE

A huge shamiana had been erected and caterers were serving dinner, but on that cold November night in 1989, very few out of the hundreds of people collected at my Wade Bhua's house in Amritsar were eating after the parliamentary election results had been declared. Victory, euphoria, and anticipation suffused the air. My father, Simranjit Singh Mann, had been released from the infamous Bhagalpur jail after five long years, and was being flown into Amritsar that night.

Amidst all this exhilaration, I stood quietly apart, too stunned to eat. I could feel nothing but intense relief—the hard month of campaigning had paid off. Papa had won the parliamentary seat in Punjab from Tarn Taran with the highest margin of votes ever in the country. He had virtually been carried by a whole wave of people determined to get him out of prison.

Fighting and winning this election seemed to have been the last hope for his release. The people were determined to exercise their vote for this man who had sacrificed his career, home, and family for the indignities the Sikhs had suffered during and after Blue Star.

I had campaigned for my father over weekends, and had even taken a few days off from school. I accompanied my aunts, Inderjit and Daljit (I will refer to them as Wade and Chhote Bhuaji) on the campaign trail and nervously faced thousands of people. The first time I spoke into the microphone all I could manage was a stammered, 'Please bring my papa home.' Later, when I realized I should have been asking for votes I would say 'Please vote for my papa so he can come home to us'; a sea of hands would go up and people would nod their heads and reassure me of their support.

At one such gathering, an old man from the crowd rose after I had made my plea, came up onto the makeshift stage, put his hand on my head and with tears in his eyes said, 'Not only will we get your father home for you, we will walk barefoot to vote for Simranjit Singh Mann.' I tried, but I couldn't stop myself and there, standing in front of a gathering of thousands, I broke down and cried. Sure enough, thousands went to the polling booths barefoot.

Back at the shamiana, everyone was piling into cars and leaving for Raja Sansi airport, where my father would finally touch home soil as a free man. In the blinding lights of the swell of cars moving to the airport I was transported back to the day Papa was arrested—29 November 1984—at Jogbani in Purnia district in northern Bihar, actually even further back to when he vanished from our sight.

As recounted by Papa:

> 'When Operation Blue Star happened on 3 June 1984, I was at Qila, my parents' home, with Bibiji and Dadji (which is what Papa called his father). I had been summoned to Chandigarh by the government for a departmental enquiry about the issuing of arms licences. My posting in Faridkot was a laugh because I had the power to recommend an arms' licence but not issue one as only the deputy commissioner of the district could do that. I was only the senior superintendent of police (SSP).
>
> I was sitting in the office of Harjit Singh, inspector general (IG), CID Punjab, answering questions, when the phone rang on his desk. 'Mann is in Punjab and right now with Bhindranwale,' said the advisor to the governor, Surendra Nath.
>
> 'Not possible, sir,' replied the IG.
>
> 'How do you know?' asked the voice on the other end of the line.

'Well, because Mr Simranjit Singh Mann is sitting in my office right across the table. So I can assure you that he is not with Bhindranwale.'

The IG hung up, exclaiming, 'This is preposterous,' and looking at me said, 'This is the height of persecution. They are after you.'

After my questioning was over, I hurried from Chandigarh to Sirhind to be home with my parents before curfew was imposed in the evening. The army was out in full force, everything was shut and once curfew was imposed, we were all prisoners wherever we were.

As soon as I reached the sanctity of my parents' home, I switched on the radio to catch the news, but had no luck. All telephonic communications had been cut off and soon the radios—except for sporadic broadcasts from the BBC—and electricity would follow. Punjab was sealed off from the rest of the world. We ate our supper in gloomy darkness and went to bed.

The next morning, while I was getting ready, BBC Radio proclaimed that Sant Jarnail Singh Bhindranwale had been killed in the Golden Temple. I stood in stunned silence and then broke down and cried. Not since the death of Virji, my elder brother, had I cried like this.

The SSP of Ropar, Mr Alam, who had trained under me in Faridkot and was my SP in the headquarters in Faridkot, came early in the morning to Qila and said, 'Sir, please get into my car. I'm taking you to the airport because the army's looking for you.'

I got into his car, saying a quick goodbye to my parents, and went straight to the Chandigarh airport, an hour away from Sirhind, from where I boarded a flight to Delhi.

At the Delhi airport, I bought some foreign newspapers, which were full of the attack on the Golden Temple. Very disturbed, I came back to Bombay (now Mumbai) and to all of you. My mind was in turmoil and I felt I could not possibly serve a government that had done this to my people.

Then I did what most devout Sikhs do—I turned to the Guru Granth Sahib to look for direction. I took a wakh (lesson for the day). It was a shabad of Guru Teg Bahadur:

'Jo nar dukh me dukh na mane. Sukh saneh aru bhaya nahi jaake', which loosely translates to:

> One who does not give importance to sorrow,
> Who does not crave happiness, and is unafraid,
> Who knows that gold and mud are the same in essence,
> who is not influenced by criticism or praise,
> Is free of greed, attachment and ego . . .

I drafted my resignation letter and the next morning, on 18 July 1984, sent it off to the President of India, ironically also a Sikh, Giani Zail Singh.

I got no reply, so I wrote another letter explaining the expediency of accepting my resignation. This time around, an officer from the Central Industrial Security Force (CISF) came to inform me that I had been dismissed from service and formally served me the dismissal notice at my office in Bombay. I handed in my service revolver amidst my shocked staff, some of whom were crying openly and some, like my personal secretary Mr Kutty, barely able to contain themselves. I thanked all of them and walked out for good.

Some days later I got word from a reliable source in the prime minister's office that the government wanted to have me eliminated. I believed the source because this person was close to the prime minister, and also an old friend of mine. Then Dadji rang and begged me to go underground for he had also heard the same. Geeta, my wife, was aghast when I told her, but finally, after much procrastination, it was decided that I should go away for a while.

I spent the first few days at a friend's house close to our own on Malabar Hill. After a few days, a Colonel Baljit Singh and his wife came and picked me up and took me to their house in Bandra since it was dangerous to stay in one place. I had to keep moving. From the Colonel's house, a transporter, Sardar Gian Singh, drove me out of Bombay in a Fiat car.

At one point along the drive, somewhere in the south of Maharashtra, we stopped for lunch at a dhaba, owned by a Sikh, who on seeing two fellow Sikhs at his dhaba was quite excited and even asked, 'Do you know that a Sikh IPS officer has resigned from service in Bombay after Operation Blue Star? What a great sacrifice he's made!'

I was nervous that Gian Singh would spill the beans and reveal my identity in his excitement, but he never let on that the Indian Police Service (IPS) officer was, in fact, right in front of him, and after a quick lunch we continued southwards. Gian Singh drove me to Madhya Pradesh to a place called Bhilai where I was to stay with a follower of Bhindranwale who ran a guesthouse for a government iron ore company. He gave me a room, which was very comfortable, but I was uneasy because government officers frequented the guesthouse.

Then he told me that Bhai Ram Singh, a former aide of Bhindranwale, was also in the same town, along with his wife and baby daughter. Would I like to meet him? I didn't know him but was very happy to meet someone from Sant Bhindranwale's camp. Bhai Ram Singh walks with a severe limp. Polio. He had been in the Golden Temple when it was attacked by the army.

On the second day of the siege, sensing things were not going well for them, Bhindranwale urged Ram Singh to get away because with his limp he wouldn't be able to got out if the situation got worse. So the day before the Sant and his companions were massacred, Ram Singh got out through a secret passage and was saved literally by the skin of his teeth—only to be later charged, along with me, with conspiracy to assassinate Prime Minister Indira Gandhi, and thrown into prison for five years. Ram Singh and I were put up together in another Sikh's house.

One morning, just as I woke up, I saw a police jeep

parked outside the neighbour's house. Ram Singh had already seen it and was in a panic. He was sure the police had come for us.

My instincts told me that we were safe, so I reassured Ram Singh. Sure enough, the police jeep left after a while.

But it was decided that we should move on. Willy-nilly, Ram Singh and I seemed to have been clubbed together. From Bhilai in Madhya Pradesh we backtracked to Nagpur. At Nagpur, we were given shelter, succour, and refuge by a Sikh transporter.

When I learnt that Indira Gandhi was to visit Nagpur, I felt it wouldn't be safe for us to be there because security would be beefed up and we could easily be arrested. So I convinced Ram Singh to leave Nagpur.

We put his wife and newborn daughter on a train back to the Punjab and we got on a train to Asansol in West Bengal, where we lived for a while before we chugged it up to Calcutta. In Calcutta, Kamikar Singh, a local Sikh leader, took charge of our safety and gave us refuge. While I was in Calcutta, my sister Dilloo Bhenji came to see me. I thought it was very brave of her to have travelled all the way from Chandigarh to meet me under the circumstances. She stayed with a friend who was a tea planter, and his wife.

For me, to have her around for those few days was wonderful. I had been missing my family and my life at home. It wasn't easy to be on the run as a fugitive. In the years that were to follow, my sister was my greatest ally and pillar of strength. She spent the next five years running around for my cause and never missed an opportunity to be with me at my appearances in court and visit me in prison. Also in Calcutta, my brother-in-law Amarinder Singh came to meet me. I did not eventually meet him—meeting him may have put me at risk, but he did leave me Rs 10,000, which was a great help and a considerable amount at the time.

For almost two months, I moved from one safe house in Calcutta to another, staying sometimes as a guest of rich Sikh transporters, smugglers, and once even at a railway colony with a Sikh engineer. The Metro was under construction at that time. Most of the contractors were Sikhs so it was safe for me to be with them. One of the areas in which I was put up was full of prostitutes and very often they would solicit me when I'd step out for a walk. I would look the other way and quicken my steps to the safety of my little temporary sanctuary.

One evening, a Sikh merchant navy officer invited me to the club. I went, but it only reminded me of home and my old life. I came back to my little room that night, miserable and quite certain that I wouldn't be going back home, or living the kind of life I was used to again.

I moved to Charan Singh's (one of the co-accused, arrested along with me under the National Security Act while we were trying to cross over to Nepal at Jogbani) flat, right next door to the police commissioner's office. I felt I was safest here—since I had been a part of the system

I knew they would never look for me right under their noses. I was cocking a snook at the system.

We had been in Calcutta for about three months when we heard that Indira Gandhi had been gunned down by her bodyguards in Delhi. It was 31 October 1984, and I was sitting in Charan Singh's flat when news about her death started trickling in. I rang up a journalist friend in Bombay who confirmed the news. My first thought was that Indira Gandhi had lived by the sword and finally died by the sword. That was it.

Then the pogroms against the Sikhs started in earnest. Many Congressmen were responsible for stirring the cauldron and for the brutal murders and rapes of innocent Sikhs. The bloodbath had started. Hindus were openly proclaiming 'Khoon ka badla khoon'.

Eventually, the men in charge of looking after me, including Kamikar Singh, head of the local gurdwara later my co-accused and fellow prisoner, decided that Calcutta wasn't safe for me any longer, and that sooner or later, the cops would find me.

So a plan was made. A great escape plan. I was to be smuggled out of the country, into Nepal, and then via Bangladesh across to Europe and eventually to America where it was thought I would be finally free. The Sikh resistance felt they could manage this.

On 29 November 1984, Kamikar Singh, Charan Singh, Bhai Ram Singh, Jaspal Singh Gorkha, and I set off in a Willys jeep at 5 a.m. Gorkha was taken along because he was a transporter and an exporter of sorts and knew all the bylanes of Kathmandu.

It was getting dark and there we were, close to the border. We had reached the small border post at Jogbani, in Purnia district in Bihar. I was very apprehensive about crossing over from Bihar, because it was a Congress-ruled state and I felt vigilance would be heightened. West Bengal, a Communist-ruled state, on the other hand, would be more sympathetic to the Sikhs after their massacre, and it would be easier to cross over to Nepal from there. But I was overruled and so the Bihar border it was.

There was no electricity in the tiny border village and the villagers had lit their lanterns. We drove past the village with Gorkha at the wheel and reached the barrier post separating India from Nepal. The barrier post looked unmanned and, joy oh joy, the post was up and just waiting for us to drive right through. I said a silent prayer.

Just as we were through, a voice said, 'Rukko rukko!' (halt, halt) and a solitary sentry came running out of the guardhouse. Gorkha panicked and brought the old jeep to a spluttering stop. And that was that. We had obviously been recognized.

The sentry led us all into a little room, and went to the wireless radio. I wasn't in disguise—stupid really—but my picture had anyway been flashed across all the border checkposts and airports so the police must have been on alert.

While we waited, I decided that I could easily run away.

The border was literally a stone's throw away and for the moment there was only one cop around, and he was busy with his wireless. I told the others, but Bhai Ram Singh pleaded that if I left, the police would definitely kill him in a fake encounter, as because of his disability, he'd never be able to run.

I sat down, and let fate run its course. Once the back-up arrived, the police took us to the local thana, and there we stayed for the night. The next morning, we were produced before a judicial magistrate, who issued a police remand. We were escorted away and kept under arrest in a rural resthouse.

Then the interrogation started and we were tied up. People from the Intelligence from Delhi arrived to interrogate me in particular—I told them the barest minimum. They wanted details about where I'd stayed, whom I'd met, and so on.

Not wanting to get anyone else into more trouble on my behalf, I kept mum while I got a few blows. When I was produced again in front of the magistrate, I said I wanted a lawyer.

'Sorry, I can't help you,' said the magistrate quite rudely.

Ram Singh, Charan Singh, and Gorkha were then separated from us and taken to lord knows where. Kamikar and I were whisked away in a separate vehicle. As I was being driven away, again lord knows where, the jeep stopped near a bamboo thicket, and I was yanked out of the jeep and led into the thicket. One of the cops said they were going to shoot me and would have, but for a Himachali ex-army man in the Bihar Armed Constabulary, who refused, saying that I was from his side of the world so his conscience did not allow him to shoot me. The others chickened out, and I was led in a state of shock, still shackled, back to the jeep.

The next morning Kamikar and I were taken to an airfield where a small eight-seater aircraft awaited us. My hands were tied so tight behind my back, that the handcuffs were jabbing into my spine horribly and I was in pain. But I didn't say a word, because that would show weakness, which I was sure they would use to their advantage. A pretty nasty Punjabi officer was in charge of us. I just grit my teeth and bore the pain. We were flown in a Beechcraft to Patna and lodged in the Home Guards resthouse. More officers from the Intelligence Bureau (IB) and Central Bureau of Investigation (CBI) arrived to interrogate us. I was not given a copy of the First Information Report (FIR) or search memo, despite asking the magistrate who was brought to the resthouse where I was detained. The superintendent of police, CID, a Kapur from Punjab, handed me the detention order no.9975/SDS B/S/-2 dated 28 November 1984 while I was in handcuffs and also made me sign what I assumed was a detention document. The officers were rude but there was no torture. Then I was flown in a Border Security Force (BSF) plane from Patna to Delhi and from there, on 5 December 1984, in a helicopter to Bharatpur.

1

OPERATION BLUE STAR was to change our lives forever.

My father was in Punjab on official work while we were all in Simla for our summer vacation. He had taken a trip to our family home in Sirhind, barely an hour from Chandigarh. He was with Ammiji and Bapuji, his parents, when the army stormed into the Golden Temple.

There was chaos in Punjab. The government had banned all press activity and sealed off Punjab to hide the atrocities it was committing. The horror that ensued is now a part of history.

The army stormed the Golden Temple on 6 June 1984 on the order of the Government of India. It unleashed its wrath on thousands of innocent devotees gathered to pay homage on the martyrdom day of the fifth guru of the Sikhs Guru Arjan Dev.

In 1982, Bhindranwale and the Akali Dal, the Sikh political party, launched the Dharam Yudh Morcha, the main aim of which was the fulfilment of the Anandpur

Sahib Resolution. Thousands joined this movement. Bhindranwale, head of the Damdami Taksal and political revolutionary, was notable for his support of the Anandpur Sahib Resolution. The Anandpur Sahib Resolution was drafted by the Akali Dal in 1973; the Resolution asks for greater autonomy to the state.

Bhindranwale made the Harmandir Sahib his headquarters in April 1980. In 1982, he along with his followers moved into a guesthouse called Guru Nanak Niwas, within Harmandir Sahib. In June 1984, this is where he was hunted down by the Indian army and slain; with him so were thousands of others who were praying within the four walls of our holiest shrine. Punjab was soon in the grip of terror.

History can decide whether Bhindranwale was right or wrong to take sanctuary along with his followers in the Golden Temple complex, which ultimately led to the massacre of thousands of innocent pilgrims by the Indian army in their attempt to get one man. Bhindranwale was slaughtered along with thousands of others, creating a gaping chasm of hatred and unrest in the already alienated Sikhs in a Hindu-dominated India. Sant Bhindranwale became an overnight martyr for the Sikhs and soon after, Indira Gandhi attained the same hallowed status when she was killed by her Sikh bodyguards.

Bhindranwale shared an ideology with my father: a separate homeland for the Sikhs. Bhindranwale paid for it with his life and my father paid for it by spending his prime years behind bars. Papa was the scapegoat the government needed; he became the hunted and finally, the trapped.

Indira Gandhi's government said that the storming of the Golden Temple by the Indian army was a spontaneous decision to flush out the militants taking sanctuary within the Golden Temple complex, after talks concerning the implementation of the Anandpur Sahib Resolution with them had broken down.

Almost thirty years later, documents released from the National Archives in London claim that the British government, headed by Margaret Thatcher, colluded with India on the deadly raid on the Golden Temple.[1] Letters between the Indian and British governments were being exchanged as early as February 1984. Thatcher even approved of two officers of the British Security Service (MI5) going to India to help Mrs Gandhi and her government plan the attack on the Golden Temple! The British government is now examining why the papers were leaked and not marked sensitive and held back. The present prime minister, David Cameron, has asked the cabinet secretary Sir Jeremy Heywood, to conduct an urgent investigation into the matter, after calls from Sikh groups for an inquiry into the alleged involvement of the British government in planning the Operation.

---

[1]Documents in the public domain.

So it comes to light that Operation Blue Star was no 'spontaneous act', as claimed by the Indian government but a well-planned and thought-out operation by the Indian army backed by the British government.

When Papa was in prison, he'd once sent me a newspaper cutting with a picture of Margaret Thatcher dressed smartly in a coat and skirt, mentioning that I should get her outfit copied and dress like her. He admired her. The recent disclosure, that she gave Mrs Gandhi the thumbs up for attacking the Golden Temple, shattered his regard for her.

Margaret Thatcher—Pa's idea of how I should dress. This is a cutting he sent me from Bhagalpur Jail.

Sikhs all over the world were upset and angry. My father at this dark hour in Indian history was in Sirhind, our ancestral village. Tempers were running high and my father's was no exception. As soon as he could, he came back to Bombay to us, we had returned earlier with Mama after our holiday in the hills and he resigned from service as an IPS officer. Always ready to call a spade a spade, he wrote to Mrs Gandhi and the President, comparing them to General Dyer and the entry of the army into the Golden Temple to the Jallianwala Bagh massacre.

As a senior police officer, serving the government that he had censured was anathema to my father. He resigned from the service to show his disapproval of what was to him a barbarous government. Sikhs from all walks of life were, as signs of protest, returning honours bestowed by the government. On 18 July 1984, Papa submitted his resignation and also sent off fiery letters to the President, ironically a Sikh himself and commander of the armed forces. He was subsequently dismissed by President Zail Singh.

A week or so later, Papa got news from his parents and from some friends from his college days who worked in the prime minister's office and home ministry that the government was about to arrest him or, worse, eliminate him because they felt that Papa may be able to organize the Sikhs into a rebellion. My father decided to go underground.

Phone No. 260371.

Sardar Simranjit Singh,
I.P.S.
Group Commandant,
Central Industrial Security Force,
Group Hqr's,
MINISTRY OF HOME AFFAIRS.

Eruchshaw Building,
249, Dr. D.N. Road
Bombay-400 001

Dated the 18th July

No. D.O. No. CISF/GHB/SSM/IPS.

Dear President Zail Singh,

It is difficult to express in words my feelings over the recent events in Punjab, and especially the desecration of the holy precincts of the Golden Templ and 37 other Gurdwaras in the Punjab by allowing the armed forces to enter these precincts, kill the faithful and destroy and pillage all that is dear and close to the heart of every Sikh. The Indian Army, with a strength of four Corps (11 Corp, 10 Corp, 1 Corp, and 2 Corp deployed) supported by Artillery (130 mm Artillery Guns) and 24 Tanks entered the holy precincts of Harmandir Sahib and the Akal Takhat Sahib was destroyed by 3.7" rocket launchers. Thirty-seven other Gurdwaras were similarly desecrated. As a Sikh you are aware that the Gurdwaras are open to all, irrespective of one's caste, creed or religion. The only force which the Sikhs have never allowed enter, without offering resistance, are the Government Forces, whether they be the Mughal, Afghan or British. The entry of any Government Force has been resisted. Baba Deep Singh, the First Jathedar of of Damdama Sahib ('Taksal' Order) offered resistance to th troops of Ahmed Shah Abdali, when the Golden Temple was blown up by the Afghans, and the holy tank desecrated by the carcasses of cows. Sant Jarnail Singh Bhindranwala, the fourteenth Jathedar of this very 'Taksal' (Order) and a great Sikh missionary, has now laid down his life, defending the sanctity of the Golden Temple.

Even during the firing at Jallianwala Bagh in 1919 the bellicose Lt.-Col. Smith favoured bombarding the town from the air, but G.A. Wathen , Principal of the Khalsa College, Amritsar, cautioned against such a drastic step. If anythi happens to the Golden Temple, he argued, the British would permanently eliminat the Sikhs, from whom the Army drew a large proportion of its soldiers. I had consistently been cautioning the Government against such stepsfor which you may kindly refer to Appendix 'A' & 'B'.

What is even more painful is that after murdering the great Sikh nationa hero, Sant Jarnail Singh Bhindranwala, the Indian Army Forces placed his body along with the bodies of Gen. Subhag Singh, Bhai Amrik Singh and Baba Thara Sin in front of the Darshani Deorhi, and displayed them to the Hindu population, which went delirious with joy. The Hindus offered sweets to the Indian Army to celebrate their great victory. It is regrettable that the Indian Army accept these sweets, and further humiliated the Sikh nation. The Indian Army, after seizing control of the Golden Temple Complex murdered several hundred Sikhs whom it had captured (which is against the Rules of Geneva Conference), looted the Tosha-Khana, and after the mopping up operations were completed, it planted several weapons on the Sikhs to prove that the Sikhs had sophisticat weapons and were making preparations to to wage a war against the Government of India m and realize their dream of independent and sovereign State. See the picture of Annexure 'C', in which the Arms are displayed, and the Indian Jawans are wearing boots within the holy precincts of the Golden Temple. You will rec that in 1919 Sir Michael O'Dwyer, the Lt. Governor of the Punjab, while defending Gen. Dyer's action, had put up a similar defence for slaying 2,000 persons of Jallianwala Bagh by stating that military action was inevitable, because the population was rising as it had done in 1857, and thus tried to ju his action. Since you are the Supreme Commander of the Armed Forces, it is my duty to inform you that Sikhs with a few weapons, which only a platoon in an Infantry Battalion has, cannot wage a war against the Government of India., and attacking them with such ferocity has only made our worst fearscome true that the Government of India is bent upon committing the genocide of the Sikhs Your statement in favour of this wild propaganda of the Government of India has poured salt on the wounds of every Sikh, whether he be in India or abroad.

The Sikhs have been patriotic and faithful to India, but the arrogance of the majority community has totally alienated them. I am attaching two letters as Annexures 'A' & 'B', addressed to the Chief Secretary, Punjab, and to show you how the Hindu Indian Government has systematically pursued a policy to annihilate the Sikhs and other minorities in India. The Army action could have been avoided had the Government been serious in finding out a negotiated settleme The Prime Minister and the Union Home Minister had given assurances that the sanctity of the holy shrines would not be violated. Unfortunately, both were telling lies all along. Mrs. Gandhi, Prime Minister, has, by this cruel action, out-done Mahmood Ghazni, and she, like Shankracharya, who eliminated the Budhist Faith in India, has, by this action, achieved a dubious reputation, though to the Hindus she has become the greatest Hindu Leader since Shankracharya.

The military action in the Punjab is only a tentative gain, for which Mrs. Gandhi will be given a fresh mandate by the Hindu majority in the ensuing General Electionsto the Parliament. However, as the President of the country and with your knowledge of Sikh history, and with your Military Advisers' knowlec of the Napoleon Spanish Campaign you could have restrained the action of your Prime Minister, and made her see the futility of this ruthless military campaign against your own people. The Government of India is far too strong , and only the paranoid, the mentally sick and the Jingoistic Hindus will believe that the Sikhs were about to wage a war against the Government of India.

Regarding the Jallianwala Bagh tragedy, the Nobel Prize Winner, Sir Rabindaranath Tagore, wrote to the Viceroy relinquishing his Knighthood, stating - "The enormity of the measures taken by the Government in Punj for quelling some local disturbances here,, with acute shock, revealed to our minds the helplessness of our positionas British subjects in India." Sixty-five years after he wrote this letter, I cannot finds words which can express my feelings any differently. What a massacre, Mr. President, and and with such a great vengeance? The soldiers of the Indian Army, who now lost their lives, are being paid One Lakh of Rupees each and other Pension benefits for their next of kin. Soldiers who lost their lives in the Wars of 1962, 1965 and 1971, were not extended those facilities. This extra bit of generosity clearly shows that the Sikhs are the biggest enemies of the Government of India, Pakistan and China having been relegated to second & third place respectively.

You have just returned from Argentina, which was recently humiliated by the British in the Falkland War. The tepid resistance put up by the Argentine soldiers was due to the factthat the Generals in Buenos Aires had killed 6,000 of their own youth in fake encounters. The Generals, as you must have observed, are behind bars and are awaiting sentences, which may bring them death. As such, this cruel and thoughtless military action in the Punjab will put Mrs. Gandhi back in the chair, but if there is a war, I will tell you very frankly that what your Government and Armed Forces have done in the Punjab and are continuing with unabated zeal, the Sikhs will not support the Government in its war effort, and the Sikh soldier, known for his intrepid resistance the world over, will not put up the type of defence , which has always saved India's integrity. The Army has already killed well over 20,000 of our youth, and the whereabouts of over 50,000 are not known. Your Prime Minister and her Generals are pursuing a policy that has already made General Dyer look too mild in comparison.

Since I strongly disapprove of this military action of the Indian Armed F into the holy precincts of our Gurdwaras and the indiscriminate killings of my people, which will eventually lead to the disintegration of our country, I tende my resignation from the Indian Police Service with immediate effect. I will henceforth work in rehabilitating the Sikh families, who have suffered from this barbaric military action, and may God help me in my endeavour. I resign withou malice towards any one, because to do so would be against the tenets of my relig

(3)

In the end, I appeal to all Sikhs to observe the 6th of every month as Martyrdom Day, and march to the residence of the Prime Minister, and offer their heads, so that she may quench her thirst for Sikh blood. By the grace of God I will present myself before her on the 6th July, 1984. Sikhs living in Provincial Headquarters should similarly present themselves before India's envoys for similar sacrifices. It is only by quenching this Lady's thirst for Sikh blood that we will survive as a separate religious entity.

With regards,

Yours sincerely,

Sd/- Simranjit Singh Mann, I.P.S.
COMMANDANT, C.I.S.F., BOMBAY.

Giani Zail Singh,
President of India, NEW DELHI.
Rashtrapati Bhavan,

Copy to:-
1. The Director-General, C.I.S.F., Lodhi Road, New Delhi.
2. D.I.G. (W/Zone), C.I.S.F., RCFI, Complex, Chembur, Bombay-400 074.

pp. 6–8: Letter from Papa to the President of India

No. I-26012/1/82/IPS
GOVERNMENT OF INDIA,
Ministry of Home Affairs

NEW DELHI-1100
Dated the 30th Jul

ORDER.

To

Shri Simranjit Singh Mann, I.P.S.,
Group Commandant, C. I. S. F.,
Eruchshaw Building,, 2nd Floor,
249, Dr. D.N. Road, Fort,
Bombay - 400 001.

Whereas the President is satisfied under sub-clause (c) proviso to Clause (2) of Article 311 of the Constitution that i interest of the security of the State, it is not expedient to h inquiry in the case of Shri Simranjit Singh Mann, I.P.S.

And whereas the President is satisfied that, on the bas the information available, the activities of Shri Simranjit Si Mann, I.P.S., are such as to warrant his dismissal from servic

Accordingly, the President hereby dismisses Shri Simran S ingh Mann, I.P.S., from service with immediate effect.

Sd/-

(C.L. BASHAL)

Under Secretary to the Government

Letter of dismissal from the Ministry of Home Affairs

And so my father disappeared while we waited.

The valet waited at the front door with my father's fine-leather slippers, for the bell that would announce his arrival. The moment Papa entered the house, he would take off his brown police oxfords, wear his slippers, walk down the tiny hall and then step onto his precious Persian carpet, which had survived Partition and been handed down to Papa by my Ammiji. In 1947, when India and Pakistan were divided, my father's family was already in Simla for the summer and as they led a hectic social life, Ammiji had brought along with her from their home (in what was soon to become Pakistan) two Persian carpets and enough silver tableware to serve a hundred people. That was the sum total of their wealth that they had salvaged!

The doorbell never rang. The valet took the slippers back to Papa's room and finally Mama said that my father was away on tour and would be back in a few days. At the time, I didn't think it was a big deal since he was often away on tour.

Before leaving, Papa had told Mama that it was prudent to go away for a bit and that he would return as soon as the witch-hunt was over. My mother was shaken to her core at the turn of events. From being a senior officer, her husband was now jobless and on the run. She was left high and dry, alone in Bombay with her three young children. That none of us perceived this till years later was a testament to her strength and stoicism, which carried her and all of us through the following years.

Mama never realized the gravity of the situation until weeks after Papa had gone underground. She had assumed it was a temporary arrangement that would last until the situation in Punjab cooled down. She was against Papa leaving and going into hiding since he'd done nothing wrong—and told him so. Papa waited for a few days, but then my grandfather cautioned him again to go away for a while because the government wanted a scapegoat and would arrest him if not finish him off altogether. Mama argued, but Bapuji was very worried—he was well aware of the witch-hunts the government was carrying out in Punjab. Finally, my mother recalls, Bapuji called her and insisted that Papa lie low for a while. 'No buts,' he told her, '*jaan hai to jahan hai*.'[2]

That was that. There was no grand plan, nothing.

The day my father never returned home from work was the day my mother's life became a living nightmare. She had thought he would be back in a week; the week turned to months and then years. 'I was like an ostrich with my head deeply buried in sand, it was the only way I could survive,' she says. She was just thirty-four years old.

---

[2] You have a life if you're alive!

At the time, my brother Emaan, my sister Nanki, and I were blissfully unaware of what was going on and that our lives were already on a roller coaster that would soon plunge us all into the scariest ride of our lives. Virji (as I called Emaan), twelve or thirteen, was at Welham Boys' School in Dehradun and unaware of all that we were going through in Bombay.

Papa had moved to a relative's house just a stone's throw away on Malabar Hill. After spending a few days there, he moved to Bandra, to a friend's house. And then to Indore. He moved constantly to avoid being found.

Mama realized that she would just have to accept the reality. She couldn't stay like an ostrich with its head buried in sand any longer. So she pulled her head out of the ground as it were, gave it a firm shake, and became a clucking mother hen with her brood to protect. Just like that she became all brisk and matter of fact.

Coming into our room one day she said, 'Girls, we have to pack up.'

'Pack? For where?' I asked.

'Yippie!' exclaimed Nanki. 'Are we going on holiday?'

I looked askance at Mama.

'Well, no,' replied Mama, in rather a clipped tone. 'We're going back home to Chandigarh for good.'

'But this is home!' I wailed. 'I don't want to go back, my friends are here, school's here, our life is here.'

No, no, we're quite happy here, thank you very much. Of course, I didn't say the last few words, as they were rude, and rudeness was unacceptable.

'Don't worry, you'll make new friends, go to a new school, be with all your cousins, won't that be fun?'

Mollified, I started dreaming of new beginnings. We had, after all, been shifting homes all our lives and moving with Papa as he got posted from place to place, so it wouldn't be such a big deal. Nanki and I were oblivious to the reality.

Mama started packing in earnest. Out came all the gunny bags, sheets of plastic, miles of ropes. Slowly, a chair, a table, a bed at a time, everything was packed. Mama had hoped that she would have at least six months or so to get her act together—perhaps we could finish our school term, and she would give in her notice at Cathedral Junior, where she taught.

But we had to leave soon since Papa had been dismissed from service. We had to give up the flat and staff. My grandfather sent the cook from Chandigarh to cook for us. Our cook, bearer, and driver had all left, albeit reluctantly. They belonged to the government. Our bai, the Maharastrian domestic help, would also leave soon.

The police trailed us everywhere we went in Bombay.

'How exciting, just like the movies,' said Mama, to assuage our fear.

When I left the house for school with my bai in the morning, one policeman would follow me all the way to school, walking just a few steps behind my bai and me. On some days, if it rained, Mama would give me the bus fare so I could take a double-decker to school—we'd still be followed by the police Ambassador car with the ridiculously simple and so obviously fake number plate 1234.

One day, we decided to go to the movies in the evening. With Papa underground and life looking grim, this may not have been the most logical thing for us to do but that's just the way it was. I think Mama saw life through rose-tinted glasses just for our sakes. So we got into our little potty-coloured Fiat, with Janak Chacha behind the wheel—my father's cousin and his new wife Parneet lived with us—and up the hill we went with our constant companions, the cops in the Ambassador 1234, behind us. They were following us to the movies—would they also sit with us and watch an English movie? We all laughed.

Mama said, 'Let's try and give them the slip.'

'Oh, let's, let's!,' screamed Nanki and I from the back of the car.

We drove down Malabar Hill, on to Marine Drive, zigzagging through the traffic, Nanki and I jumping up and down on our seats with excitement, craning our heads around to see if we'd lost them. We turned towards Colaba, and 1234 stayed close behind us all the way to the cinema hall. The cops didn't watch the movie with us but sat patiently in their car, waiting for us to come out, and then tailed us all the way home.

The next day, the gas cylinder had to be returned to the gas depot. With no one now to do it for her, Mama and Parneet Chachiji set off to return it, cops following. When they reached the depot, Mama got out of the car, strode up to the Ambassador, and knocked on the window. The policeman literally jumped out of the car. So far we had not acknowledged each other's constant presence.

Mama said, 'Since you're here and have nothing better to do than follow us around, you may as well help me unload the gas cylinder and drop it off inside.'

She was angry. Nanki and I weren't with her so her guard had dropped. The policeman, taken by surprise, followed her, got the cylinder out of the boot and carried it into the agency.

With no gas, and the electricity, water, and flat soon to go, we were in quite a hard place. Nandu, our cook from home, had to make do with a kerosene stove to cook our food.

My Uncle Janak, had found alternative accommodation. His wife would go back with us to Chandigarh for the time being.

'I'll huff and I'll puff and blow your house in,' said the Big Bad Wolf.

'Not by the hair on my chinny chin chin,' said the frightened piggy. 'I'll not let you in.'

Mama was lying in our bed reading out *The Three Little Pigs* to Nanki. It read so much like our situation. Even now this story gives me goosebumps.

In our lives, the big bad wolf was the government and the strong and wise piggy who kept her house safe was Mama. Our room was bare. Everything was packed except the bed, which would be packed the next morning and along with everything else, loaded onto trucks and sent to Chandigarh, where we were also headed in just another day. The next day was to be our last in Bombay.

Teddy Phuparji (uncle) and my cousin Hari Vir arrived from Chandigarh via Indore where Phuparji had met Papa and was carrying a couple of letters from Papa to Mama. He handed the letters over to Mama, who hastily read them and then stuffed them into her bag. Teddy Phuparji and Hari Vir had come to help us and to drive the Fiat back to Chandigarh. We were all to spend the last night in the home of my parents' friends.

After my uncle and cousin had washed up, Mama, Nanki and I left the flat with them to say farewell to some friends. The plan was to meet them and then go down the hill to a frankie parlour for lunch. When we came out of the building after meeting and saying goodbye to our friends, we noticed that the building was surrounded by police. We were asked to get into our car and follow the police down to the thana.[3] Teddy Phuparji drove our car with Hari Vir in front, squashed in with a cop. Mama, Nanki, and I got in the back. While driving to the thana, Mama realized that in her bag were the letters from Papa that she had hastily put in earlier in the morning. Nothing wrong with that, except that one of them disclosed his whereabouts and if her bag were searched, the police would discover the letter and be able to find Papa and then nab him.

So stealthily, she put her hand into her bag and bit by bit tore up the letters, never looking down or into her purse, thinking no one would notice her throwing the tiny scraps out of the car door as she opened it, released the bits of shredded letters, and shut the door again firmly, pretending that the door hadn't been shut properly.

Months later Nanki narrated this little incident to her teacher in school, who in turn told my mother. Nanki had said, 'Mama thought no one saw but I did; she tore up some paper and threw it out of the car when the police had us. You see, ma'am, my father is in a secret.'

So someone had seen Mama, but that someone kept her little mouth firmly shut until months later, never breathing a word till she found her own confidante in Farida Baria, a family friend and her teacher at school.

---

[3] Police station

Back at the thana, we were kept sitting for hours in a little room. Teddy Phuparji was taken away for questioning.

Mama lost her cool and told the officer in charge that they could not keep us there indefinitely and that she had two small children whose lunch time was long past. She said that they could do what they liked but she was leaving with her kids right away.

Surprisingly, the cops let us go. We were escorted back to our now empty flat. But instead of leaving us at the entrance to our building, the policemen, lots of them, followed us up to the flat and searched for God alone knows what. A few of them started opening the bare cupboards in the tiny kitchen. Mama flung open a kitchen drawer and yelled, 'Are you sure he's not in there? Have a closer look.'

The police withdrew and left. We asked if they had search warrants, which they did not. We no longer had the protection of the law either—were we stateless people?

The next day, an article in a newspaper said that Simranjit Singh Mann's flat had been searched and incriminating documents had been found. Where so many documents were found in an entirely empty flat is still a mystery.

By the evening Teddy Phuparji still hadn't come home from the police station. Mama was sick with worry. The trucks had to be loaded and dispatched, and we were to board the Bombay Deluxe the next morning and leave for Ambala. Where was her brother-in-law?

At her wits' end, Mama picked up the phone and called the chief of police, Mr Rebeiro, and explained her predicament. He was apologetic and assured Mama a safe passage through his state, Maharashtra, and that Teddy Phuparji would be released from police questioning immediately.

Teddy Phuparji came home shortly afterwards and we left to spend our last night at our friends' home. We were too tired and stunned by the day's events to register that our life in Bombay and our carefree days were over.

My mother, aunt, five-year-old sister Nanki, and I reached Ambala after a long and tiring journey with our bags and baggage in August 1984. Many questions were troubling me. I wanted to know where our father was. Questions that remained unanswered. The grown-ups wouldn't tell us anything. Nanki thought we were back in Punjab for our summer holidays, but I knew all was not well.

At Ambala station we were met by our car. A police jeep was standing next to it and followed us all the way to Chandigarh. It was a little unnerving to be escorted by the police after such a long journey, but not too disquieting as we had become used to it in Bombay.

In Chandigarh, we settled into a somewhat disorderly family existence. For us, the children, it was rather exciting to be living with our aunt Subhagya Taiji and cousins Girimere Vir and Bhavani Bhen—we had never all lived under one roof before. Taiji is one of the gentlest and kindest of women and she opened her house and heart to us. The rest of the family rallied around and we were never short of affection. My Taiji is the widow of my father's older brother. Our home was called the henhouse—the boys, Emaan and Girimere, were away at boarding school.

Even with all the family rallying around us, we were a little insecure and lost. I missed my father, didn't know where he was, and resented him for bringing so much upheaval into our lives, a new home, new school new friends, no father around—it was all a bit bewildering.

In October 1984, soon after we'd moved to Chandigarh, Indira Gandhi was assassinated and in retaliation for her death, Sikhs were subsequently massacred in Delhi and other parts of the country. One heard terrible tales of arson and murder. Chandigarh was relatively unaffected though the fear was palpable even to us children. As we were in a house full of women and children, the family was apprehensive about our safety. Taiji and Mama, searching the house for protective weaponry, came upon a ladies' pistol—my grandmother's—with a rusty old bullet, and a khukri (knife) without a blade. Taiji's concept of keeping anything safe was to put it under her pillow. So these delightfully decrepit pieces of equipment meant to protect us went under there. I think we also all slept in the same bed, mercifully not under her pillow!

Those were terrible days. The only source of news was the little that was aired by the BBC. The adults talked in hushed tones—we heard a snippet here and a snatch there; only a fraction of the horrors that were taking place everywhere.

2

RETURNING FROM A trip to meet the boys in Dehradun few months later, Taiji and Mama heard of my father's arrest when they stopped for a tea break at Paonta Sahib Gurdwara. The driver read about the arrest in the newspaper.

When they returned home, my mother very gently broke the news to me in the drawing room with the old threadbare maroon Persian carpet.

The memory of me standing on the carpet and hearing the news is frozen in my mind. The carpet was one of Papa's most precious possessions—his mother had managed to salvage it during Partition and had handed it down to him—and he had placed a thin strip of cloth on it for us to walk on.

I had never seen my mother cry before, but now with tears in her eyes she told me I had to be very strong. I realized that this was what both my mother and my father needed most from me then. I remember asking my mother, 'Now what?' and she said, 'I don't know, but we'll manage somehow.'

That's how we survived, one day at a time.

Sheer determination carried the family through those trying times. For three whole weeks no one knew where my father was. The government would not tell us, it was almost as if he had disappeared without a trace. Everyone was frantic with worry, calling on any resources that would help, to find out if he was even alive.

We finally learnt that Papa had been detained in the Bharatpur jail in Rajasthan. Once they knew where he was, my mother, grandparents, and bhuas rushed to meet him.

Initially they weren't allowed access but were assured by the jail authorities that he was fine, that he soaked in the sun every day (it was December), and that he was well looked after.

When they finally did get to meet him, as my mother recounts, she couldn't believe her eyes. He seemed to have aged ten years; he was pale, emaciated, and cold. For an entire month he had been incarcerated in his cell with no bedding or warm clothes. So much for soaking up the sun.

My father was left in solitary confinement in a 'condemned' cell—a cell where an accused awaits the death penalty—in the Bharatpur jail under the National Security Act (NSA), which allows the Indian government to hold a person for twelve months without trial. He steadfastly refused to submit to the trumped-up charge of conspiracy to assassinate Mrs Indira Gandhi.

During this period, Ram Jethmalani, one of the country's most eminent lawyers, met Papa in jail. He remarked that he had expected to see a much younger man, as his appearance belied his actual age. Within the span of a couple of months of imprisonment and severe torture, he had indeed aged. In the first quarter of 1985, Ram Jethmalani took up Papa's case on humanitarian grounds. Amiji pleaded with him, and he decided to defend Papa, charging only a token fee, just a fraction of his usual fee. He was India's most expensive lawyer at the time.

The first time I met him was at Chhote Bhuaji's house, where a game of bridge was in progress, after he'd taken on Papa's case. He seemed unassuming, but as one watched him argue over the years, we realized just how impressive he was.

Letter from Mama to Papa

15 December,
Chandigarh,

Dear Simran,

I'm taking a chance that this may reach you. God willing it will. Everyone here is fine. A sub-inspector from Bassi informed us that you were in Bharatpur. We're trying

> our level best to see you. It seems it will be a slow process. This is just to say there is so much prayer and love for you from everyone—along with more practical matters being seen to. Everyone is trying to do their little bit. We had such a shock when we read about it in the newspaper. But of one thing I'm sure—Waheguruji is around us and He will stand by always. There's nothing I can say, as this, I'm sure, will be censored. Our chins are up—keep smiling, love from one and all—impossible to list everyone,
>
> Yours
>
> Geeta

Papa did receive this letter—it's stamped as received.

What an act of faith it was for Mama to write such an encouraging and cheery note. Little did she know then that she would have to keep up the bravado for five more years.

In Papa's first letter from the Bharatpur jail written to Mama on 17 December 1984, he asks her for some fresh clothes and warm underclothing as 'it does get bitterly cold in the cell'.

Papa writes:

I have not had the sun since I reached here. I say my prayers very often and the saving grace is that they let me have my 'gutka' [a prayer book small enough to carry around], the one which I've always carried and since there's no place to keep it other than the floor, I keep it in my shirt pocket and even go to sleep with it in my pocket, always next to me . . . I have made friends with two pigeons, who now walk up to my cell, and I give them a few of the grams that are given to me. In fact they're quite friendly and sometimes even come through the iron-spiked gate of my cell. There's a cat too, a black-and-white striped one which visits my cell whenever it's looking for a meal . . .

RATS—I have no intention of befriending them—there are plenty of! Since the jail is quite far out of the city, I do hear the call of the partridge and ducks flying in and out of the bird sanctuary. They dip their wings to say hello to me and fly merrily by. There are peacocks too; I hear their most annoying call but never get a glimpse of the majestic bird. Oh! And monkeys visit me often too. I'm thankful that the jail authorities allow me to see one of their gods, though the darshan of the Surya (sun) is never allowed!

I have made out a routine for myself and I follow it quite strictly or one could go loony. God is my only companion and He does keep me company and looks after me. The elections appear to have reached a pitch and I can hear the various candidates extol their virtues over the mikes, but who has an edge is difficult to say as I can only hear the noise, which all of them have managed to make quite a bit of and in that sense I could say that if that's the criteria for spotting the winner, then each one has as good a chance as the other!

I am not allowed any reading material and have been deprived of my watch, so it's difficult to tell the time, date, or the day. I don't even know if this letter will pass through, though I have written the barest minimum in conformity to the rules conveyed to me verbally.

Give my love and respects to my parents and my parents-in-law—sorry for the formality but this is according to the rules here. Keep your chin up and keep smiling—whether the weather be good (or cold) we'll weather the weather, no matter what the weather, whether we like it or not.

Goodbye and cheerio with lots of love,

Yours FE . . .[1]

P.S. Do give my regards to the staff.

Though Papa dates this letter 17 December the prison authorities date it 14 December. Whether Papa got his

[1] Forever

dates mixed up as he didn't have a watch or the authorities got the date wrong, one can't say, but one thing is for sure: the letter was censored as bits were blotted out with blue ink. Pa tried to keep our spirits up in all the letters he wrote; they're all positive and informative about random things. When I read through them now, I often feel a large lump in my throat—to think that he wrote little anecdotes about his life in prison, spinning them into stories to amuse us, while for him it must have been so very difficult.

Drawing for Papa in prison. Made by Nanki aged 5.

3

PAPA WAS SHUT in solitary confinement on 5 December 1985, in a tiny ten-by-eight foot cell, and not let out until 20 December 1985, when he was allowed out into a small courtyard outside the cell for a part of the day before he was locked up again at 6.30 p.m. in solitary confinement. Searchlights were kept on so Pa could be kept under observation at all times. A search beam was trained on him all night, which damaged his eyesight permanently. The suffocatingly small cell had a tap and a hole for a WC. Pa ate, bathed, slept, and defecated in this tiny area. The ventilators in the cell had been sealed.

The torture started on 6 December, a day after Papa's arrival at Bharatpur Jail. He was taken to a cell, where electrodes were attached to his big toe and penis, and an electric current was then passed through. His blood pressure was periodically taken by a doctor. Tufts of hair from his beard were yanked out, leaving a gaping bald patch on his chin, which he later handed over to a

Mr Bakshi, who was in charge of the interrogation team.

Pa informed the jail superintendent, Mr Upadhya, about the torture. Mr Upadhya replied, 'It is good for your health as it will keep your wits sharp.' Papa then wrote a letter to the Rajasthan home secretary, which he doubted would ever reach him.

As recounted by Papa:

> The government slapped a National Security Act (NSA) case on me; that would allow them to keep me in long detention. Otherwise, with no proof against me, I would have had to be immediately released.
>
> I was flown to Bharatpur, in Rajasthan, from Patna. Bharatpur, of the bird sanctuary fame. My home now would be the Bharatpur jail, solitary confinement, in a death cell, hardly a sanctuary for me. . .
>
> I was taken to this particular place because in Rajasthan the period I could be held under the NSA was two years whereas everywhere else in India the maximum time the state could detain a person was one year. This draconian law gives the state the power to hold a person without trial, which defies the laws of justice.
>
> I was led in through the imposing gates of the prison, first through one gate into a little courtyard with offices on either side. The barred gate behind me was locked and another in front of me opened. I was ushered through

FOR OFFICIAL USE		
INVESTIGATIONS		
DATE	RADIOLOGICAL	No
		X-
		X-
		X-
		X-
		X-
		X-
		X-
		X

DATE	LABORATORY	No.

नेहरू चिकित्सालय 024020

स्नातकोत्तर चिकित्सा-शिक्षा एवम् अनुसंधान संस्थान, चण्डीगढ़

CR. OF 01 POSTGRADUATE INSTITUTE OF MEDICAL EDUCATION & RESEARCH CHANDIGARH

OUT PATIENT TICKET

DATE: 8/12/[illegible] CR. No. Service

NAME: Sh. S. S. [illegible] MANN

AGE: [illegible]

INCOME Rs. [illegible] PAYING/NON PAYING LOCAL/OUT STATION

PROVISIONAL DIAGNOSIS: [illegible] 1. Recurrent [illegible] 2. [illegible] 3. Osteoarthritis, tendonitis

DATE & INITIAL | TREATMENT AND INVESTIGATIONS ORDERED

PAID Rs. 5/-

Recent Regional:

Severe dyspnoea occurring off & on since 2-3 yrs.

Received several electric shocks to genitalia while in police jail. This caused severe dyspnoea & choking & was unbearable.

Was also physically tortured — pulling of hair, [illegible] by [illegible] & [illegible] his knees (Physical trauma).

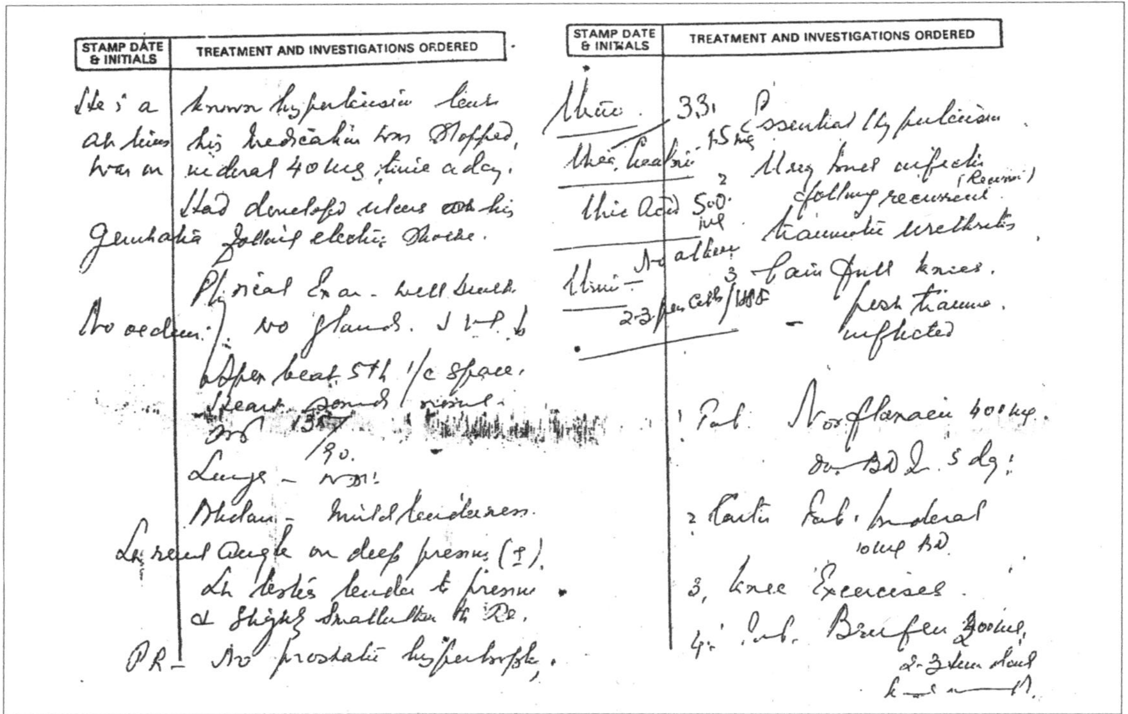
STAMP DATE & INITIALS	TREATMENT AND INVESTIGATIONS ORDERED
He is a	known hypertensive but
at times	his medication was stopped,
was on	Inderal 40 mg twice a day.
	Had developed ulcers on his
Genitalia	following electric shocks.
	Physical Exam - well built.
No oedema.	No glands. JVP [illegible]
	Apex beat 5th i/c space.
	Heart sounds normal.
	BP 135/90.
	Lungs - NAD.
	Abdomen - mild tenderness.
Lt renal angle	on deep pressure (?).
	Lt testis tender to pressure
	& slightly smaller than Rt.
PR -	No prostatic hypertrophy.

STAMP DATE & INITIALS	TREATMENT AND INVESTIGATIONS ORDERED
Urea 33.	Essential hypertension.
Urea creatinine 1.5 mg	Urinary tract infection (Recurrent)
Uric Acid 5.0 mg	following recurrent traumatic urethritis.
Urine - No albumin 2-3 pus cells/HPF	Painful knees - post trauma inflicted
	1. Tab. Norflox 400 mg BD x 5 days.
	2. Caution Tab. Inderal 10 mg BD.
	3. Knee Exercises.
	4. Tab. Brufen 400 mg 2-3 times daily

Top doctor at the post graduate institute veries the torture papa went through at a check up shortly after his release that and once I was through, it was immediately locked.

I was now within the prison confines. To my surprise, I was not taken to the prisoners' barracks but beyond them.

After a short walk, we arrived at a row of five or six abandoned little cells. I was taken into one of these and unceremoniously locked up. The room was about seven feet long and about six feet wide, with a raised cement platform to one side and a hole in the ground, with a tap above it on the wall. The door was of iron with bars. There was no window. The cell had been given a quick lick and a promise of paint, especially for me, I rightly presumed. This was to be my new home. Charming.

I sat down on the platform and waited. It was bitterly cold. The freshly whitewashed walls were damp and the hard platform I sat on didn't help. After a few hours, a guard arrived, unlocked the door and handed me my meagre supper and a coarse woollen blanket, and without saying a word locked me up again and left.

I couldn't eat, not even a tiny morsel—I was paralysed with fear and the cold. Eventually, I just curled myself into the blanket and fell into a fitful sleep.

In the morning I woke up to a noisy clattering. The sound came from the pigeons on the tin roof.

I spent a while trying to chase them away but they would keep coming back. I discovered that the hole in the floor in the corner of the room was to be my WC. And the single tap my shower. No question of hot water of course.

A guard came by again with my breakfast.

'Why am I being kept here?' I asked.

'Don't know, but you are in a death cell,' he said and left.

So I had been put into a condemned prisoners' cell already, without trial, waiting to be hanged I supposed.

The next time the guard came around I asked to see a doctor.

'Tomorrow, perhaps,' said the guard, 'I'll inform the jailer of your request.'

He left another meal for me and took away the uneaten plate of food without another word.

But I guess he informed the jailer that I hadn't touched my food and the next morning the doctor arrived.

I was relieved to see him. He was a kindly man and prescribed me Inderal, which I needed for high blood pressure, and also advised that fruit be given to me every day.

I started taking my medicine and felt a little better.

The loneliness was getting to me. All I had to do the whole day was chase pigeons from my little cell, which only left me more alone. I thought of suicide, I mulled it over in my head—it would be easy, I was half-dead already from the cold and not eating enough and most of all, from the loneliness.

I had not been let out once from the cell. The cold damp walls and hard floor were blurring into one dark hole in my mind. The actual hole, my pot, distressed me no end. I hated squatting, in fact I couldn't. I needed an English-style pot.

That probably should have been the least of my worries but it all added up and I felt I just couldn't handle the struggle any more. I fell asleep with these ideas in my head.

But something saved me.

The next morning I woke up feeling better and more focused. I realized that with my suicidal thoughts I would be playing right into the hands of the government. After all, wasn't that exactly what they wanted, to kill me? Putting me in a death cell, dark, cold, and dingy with no amenities, not even bedding save for the crude blanket, were all ways of breaking me. Once I realized this, a new determination awoke in me and I decided I would beat them yet.

First things first: I had to have a routine, otherwise I would go stark raving mad. On the damp peeling wall, I started a calendar. With my fingernail I would make a line for each day I spent in my cell. Then I paced my steps. I would walk almost the length of my body one way and then a step further the other way. Six feet by seven. Walk and pray, walk and pray.

In the mornings I would be given a white enamel mug full of tea and some boiled chickpeas to eat with it. The harder chickpeas I started saving and using as markers. For every prayer I said, I would put aside one marker. Every

Chopai Sahib (a prayer to ward off evil and give strength, composed by our tenth guru, Guru Gobind Singh, my idol) I recited made me stronger. At night to ward off the cold—it was freezing—I would sit under the tap of running cold water till my body was numb and finally, warm.

True to his word the doctor started sending me extra fruit with my Inderal. More than the odd apple, I looked forward to the newspaper bag in which it came. I would take out the apple or orange and then carefully tear open the bag and read the old newspaper, savouring each written word, reading every snippet on the small scrap of paper and then imagining the bits that were cut and left out of my little carry bag. After I had read and reread the paper, I would lay it out on the hard platform, my bed, and eventually, I had myself a mattress of newspaper bags. I had read somewhere that vagabonds in New York slept on park benches wrapped in old newspapers to keep themselves warm. A fine lesson in necessity being the mother of invention!

4

MY FATHER HAD been transferred to various parts of Punjab before we shifted to Bombay. (Just as my mother's garden would begin to look presentable, we'd have to move.) And until Bombay, we knew very little about our parents; they had their own lives and we were happy in our own little world of members of our staff and their children. Virji and I—Nanki was born a few years later—had a very 'proper' upbringing (with children, as the proverb went, 'meant to be seen and not heard').

Papa was a dichotomy—a stern, tall, uniformed figure by day, but with his hair down) and great fun to be with in the evenings and over weekends.

My earliest memories are of Ferozepur, where Papa was posted when I was about five years old. We lived in a huge white colonial bungalow within a massive compound, with a big lawn, a long drive on one side and a huge vegetable garden on the other, behind which was a block of quarters for the staff. Virji and I were enrolled in the local convent school, and every morning we would ride pillion behind the orderlies on their bicycles and be taken to school.

My brother was always up to some mischief and since I was his tail, I followed him and got punished for doing nothing more than hero worship. Once he tried to run away from school and came to fetch me from my class; without a second thought I ran out behind him. We didn't get far—we had to duck into a sweeper's closet to avoid a teacher in the corridor. We were caught crouched in the small airless cupboard by the sweeper who marched us to the principal's office, where we were soundly thrashed, and my mother was summoned.

A year later we moved to Faridkot. My brother and I learnt how to ride. The police lines were next to our house, and every morning two huge police horses would arrive with two constables to teach us.

Our horses were called Harbans Kaur and Laddu. I was about five and a half years old then, and Virji and I had riding lessons every morning. My brother picked up horseriding quickly and because the sahib, our trainer, was always singing Virji's praises to my father, I would put my fear aside and mount my horse, heart in my mouth. I hoped that Papa would notice what a good rider I was, at least as good as, or perhaps even better than, Virji.

After our morning ride we would be scrubbed and bathed by the bai and packed off to school.

Riding lesson in Faridkot

In 1979, while we were still living in Faridkot, Virji was admitted to Welham Boys' School in Dehradun. I was distraught at the thought of my brother going away without me for months together. On the morning he was to leave, no one woke me, fearing the scene I'd create. But I did awaken and as my parents had feared, proceeded to kick up a happy row. Nevertheless, off drove Mama and Virji, down the circular drive, leaving me behind. Papa took one look at me screaming and sent me off to the quarters with the bai.

After Virji left for school, I looked forward even more to visits from Pavan Bhen, my uncle's elder daughter from his first marriage. We enjoyed spending time together even though she is much older than I am.

We would spend the mornings riding. Pavan Bhen had a bad fall from the horse once and was dragged home with her foot stuck in the stirrup. It didn't put her off; after a few days she was back in the saddle.

Virji and I aged 7 and 5 in the lawn at Faridkot

Posing for the camera with Pa in Faridkot

In the afternoons we would often sit around the fire in Papa's study playing dumb charades or cards, a can of condensed milk doing the rounds between us. On one such afternoon, when Papa was also with us, we decided to dress him up in one of Pavan Bhen's skirts. First we made him wear a long satin flowing skirt, then we stuffed a pair of rolled-up socks down his tee and finally, plaited his hair and painted his lips a bright red. He was a sight to behold, and we enjoyed every minute of it. Hysterics followed!

I was a piping little sparrow of a child, happy to tell stories. That same evening Papa had to attend a police parade and I was taken along. He sat, looking handsome and every inch the police officer, with the district commissioner on one side of him and I on the other side. Everyone was sitting silently, waiting for the parade to begin when I decided something must be said to perhaps entertain the DC sahib as it was bad etiquette to have prolonged silences in company. So, remembering my manners, I leant across my father and proceeded to recount the afternoon's activity in complete detail and in Punjabi. 'Te thaunu pata hai ji, asi na, Papa nu Pavan Bhen di satin di skirt pahnai, fir asi lipstick lagi te awnna diya gutta banayi. Te pata hai, juraba nu gol gol karke auna di T-shirt che pa dite. Papa bilkul kuri lag rahe si . . .!'[1] After I finished my story, there was pin-drop silence, the DC staring with his jaw dropped at Papa. Some hemming and hawing ensued. Papa never took me along with him again for an official event.

Papa got his own back at me many years later in Bombay. I was eleven or twelve years old then, and walking home with my girlfriends. Papa and Mama saw us from the balcony. They waved to us and we said we were coming up. Mama had just been shopping and had bought some cotton skirts for herself to wear on our upcoming trip to Goa. When

---

[1] And do you know, we dressed Papa up in Pavan Bhen's satin skirt, then we painted his lips with lipstick and plaited his hair, and then we put a couple of rolled-up socks into his T-shirt. Papa looked just like a girl!

we rang the doorbell, to my horror and embarrassment, Papa stood there in a skirt, holding the door open and inviting us to enter in a falsetto, coquettish voice.

'Hello girls, do come in,' he simpered.

I did not know where to hide. My friends weren't sure if they should be shocked or should laugh. My mortification was complete.

Nanki, my younger sister, was born when we were in Faridkot. My mother went to her parents' home in Chandigarh for the delivery and I was left behind with Papa since school was in session. I happily stayed back, enjoying having my father to myself.

Papa told me that since Mama was away I would be mistress of the house and his hostess, which delighted me. I took the role very seriously. Prem Masi and Masarji, my maternal grandaunt and uncle, lived close by, and I often stayed over with them. One evening I decided to invite them for dinner. Since I was the hostess, I dressed up in one of my mother's chiffon saris and a pair of her heels and came down for dinner. Prem Masi, Masarji, and Papa, keeping very straight faces, complimented me on my sari. Unfortunately, I fell asleep literally over my plate at dinner and had to be carried up to bed by the bai.

In Faridkot one of the biggest treats was to go for a ride along the canal either on bicycle or horses. Canals are one of the features that break the monotony of the otherwise flat, great plains of the Punjab. Life flourishes along the canals. The tall trees along the banks are numbered by the government and wear white stockings; they're whitewashed to about two feet from the base of their trunks to protect them from white ants. The branches of these trees stretch over the water as well as provide shade to the kaccha roads that run along the canal. Kingfishers perch patiently atop branches, waiting to swoop down on a passing fish and make a meal of it. The thickets along the banks are home to wild boar, deer, partridges, bulbuls, shikras, egrets, koels, crow pheasants, lapwings, barbets, babblers, and chestnut bitterns. The hollows of the trees are home to the spotted owlet.

All this we were taught by Papa on rides, either bicycle or horse, and walks along the canals. Quaint gurdwaras and old English resthouses dotted canal roads and banks. Both have in recent times been vandalized by the government and the Shiromani Gurdwara Prabandhak Committee (SGPC)—resthouses by the former and the gurdwaras by the latter have been rebuilt into huge, tiled monstrosities, losing the charm and ethos of the ages they epitomized.

I remember vividly a happy canal incident involving Papa's most beloved mutt, Otto von Bismarck, named for the famous general, who Papa admired. Virji and I were cycling along a canal in Faridkot, while Papa, Mama, and Otto walked behind us when Otto went charging down the steep bank into the water—whether he was hot, chasing a bird or just being his mutt self, we never did know. The current was strong and Otto couldn't swim back to the bank and was being carried along by the racing current, still afloat somehow. After much franticness, the orderlies were commanded to take off their turbans, which were tied together and one of these hapless, brave men was lowered into the surging water to retrieve the idiot retriever.

Papa insisted that Otto's purpose in life was to be a gun dog, even if Otto didn't know it. He was trained and was diligently taken on shikaar to prove himself. On one such shikaar, Papa shot a partridge on the wing—the bird was injured but speedily disappeared into the cotton fields. Otto was sent to flush it out—which he obediently did—but when Papa tried to get the bird out of his mouth, Otto wouldn't let go. He'd forgotten his training. Papa was getting hotter under the collar with every minute of abject disobedience. Finally, the local shikaari who had accompanied Papa and his friend and stood by watching in amusement, asked if he could help. Papa huffed 'go ahead' in defeat. The shikaari blew into Otto's ear and out fell the partridge!

The partridge, or what was left of it, was cooked over the bonfire and as punishment, Otto was not given even a morsel.

Those were idyllic days when we sat around the fire, playing happy families.

Papa met Sant Jarnail Singh Bhindranwale for the first time in Faridkot. This is what he says:

(1)

Darling Pitsi, Fateh. 12th Aug. 10

You asked what was my first impression when I met Sant Jarnail Singh Bhindranwala (SJB hereafter)?

We were in Faridkote in 1979. He, along with his ramshackle retinue ('I say this because at this period of time it was not well armed and possessed only an elementary .12 bore shot guns) came to meet us at our home. He didn't seem to be in a firm state of mind as only that year (1979) the Nirankaris, a schismatic faith of the Sikhs had 'gunned down' several Sikhs in Amritsar on the day of the Baisakhi. There was an Akali government in office and Sardar Parkash Singh Badal was the Chief Minister. Instead of arresting the Nirankari Baba - Gurbachan Singh the Akali government had given him safe passage out of the Punjab and not arrested him. S.J.B was in sorrow as he was the main spiritual leader that day in Amritsar when 13 Sikhs were gunned down. He was more sorry that an Akali government had escorted the

(2)

Baba out. Theirs was the state, a humiliating one for SJB that day when he came to see me.

As he got out of his vehicle, I walked up to receive him and escort him to our drawing room. It was the first I had seen and met of SJB. He was a tall thin and slender man, dressed in the traditional toga of the Damdami Taksal, the Sikh seminary founded by Baba Deep Singh, your family's progenitor and a great Sikh martyr who won martyrdom defending the holy precincts of Darbar Sahib (Golden Temple) when the Afghan marauder Ahmed Shah Abdali invaded its holy precincts in 1762. SJB's toga came down to a little under his knees. It was white, well washed. As shoes he wore a 'desi juti' which he could easily take off when the occasion demanded as, as per his spiritual duties he had to take them off oft and on. He wore his little kirpan, a traditional Sikh dress, that hung ~~around~~ down

(3)

Till his left hip. Surprisingly he didn't carry the customary three foot long sword, which is the sign of a senior Sikh Jathedar. Instead he carried a silver arrow, about two feet in length, thick and pretty heavy. It obviously couldn't be shot from a bow and was only symbolic, in keeping with his exalted position of heading the Damdami Taksal. He wore a dark blue turban, again in the traditional style of the Taksal as did all his retinue who were all dressed in his (SJB's) fashion. They were all young. Tough, tall and good looking.

SJB wore no smile. He was serious. I felt awkward. His face was grim and serious. He had a flowing black beard. He was young, perhaps a few years younger to me. He was handsome. Had an aquiline nose and patrician features. Eyes were dug deep into his forehead. Eyelids not fully open. His physiognomy was that of a hawk. Alert and anxious. But what struck me most were his long arms and hands, the fingers of which went

(4)

down a little below his knees.
He asked two of his retinue to accompany him. One of them held a (garvi ਗੜਵੀ) (find out the word in English) full of water and the other was his body guard or perhaps his confidant, who I later learnt would record, after our meeting, the minutes of what transpired. He was extremely well mannered and took off his desi juti before he tread on our Persian carpet and so did his two escorts. I felt embarrassed as we don't take off our shoes, though in some European homes shoes are taken off before entering the drawing room.

The preliminaries were that Anwar brought in a tray of glasses filled with water, which were first put before SJB, who politely refused and then his two followers followed suit. Then I asked whether he would drink milk as that is the polite thing to ask by a host of his exalted spiritual guests. Again he politely declined the offer and so did his two men. After that

(5)

Anwar brought in two silver kaulis filled with raisins and almonds. This is again in customary with the entertainment of high dignitaries of the spiritual order. SJB had a few raisins and a few almonds, so did his escorts. That was in keeping with the politeness not that they needed to eat them. Later I learnt that the guy carrying the "garvi" was his man Friday, what Anwar was and what Lalit is to me. He is known as the garwai ([illegible]) They had refused to drink water or milk as it was not served by a baptised Sikh. Moreover the two liquids were being served in glass tumblers. Sikhs of the Taksal used only iron utensils in which their food was cooked and drank and ate out of plates and glasses of the same metal. I also learnt later that my honoured guests would not eat of, or drink of food cooked by a non-Sikh. We had a Hindu cook. That was certainly taboo because in the strict religious order of the Taksal food and drink can't be taken, cooked or

6

served by a Hindu as it's firmly believed that Hindus smoke and chew tobacco, both strictly forbidden by the Sikh faith.

We didn't talk very much as we didn't know one another before. It was a meeting to prelise one another and how much we could trust one another. I broke the ice by saying how bad and sad the Narankari episode was. SJB nodded approval and accepted my commiseration. I said I would be helpful and he need feel no anxiety in my district, which was also his, hailing from a village Rodé, not very far from Faridkote. Meeting over, I bid him adieu and saw him to his car. I thought I'd met a sincere man, committed to his religion and nation. After that our association and friendship grew.

That's as much I can recollect of my first meeting with SJB.

With lots of love!

Loving Papa.

During these years, we spent our summer holidays up in the hills. One month in Simla with Nana and Nani and my maternal family and a little over a month up in Dalhousie, in our summer home perched atop a hill surrounded by a dense deodar forest and overlooking the snow-clad peaks of the Pir Panjal range. The forest was home to the Himalayan sloth bear, leopard, wild pheasants, and us!

In the 1970s and 1980s there was no road, only bridle paths leading up to the cottage—we now have a kuccha road and can drive up to the house. After the ten-hour drive in the sweltering heat of June, during which the car invariably broke down, we would walk up the last 400-odd metres. Now it takes seven hours at the most, including a lunch stop at McDonalds, but in those days, there were no petrol pumps in or around Dalhousie, so once we'd made our way up, the car would be parked neatly hugging the hillside, and there it rested, covered with a tarpaulin for the entire duration of the trip.

We would walk everywhere, Papa often carrying Nanki in a knapsack when she was too small to walk. We would jump into bed with our parents early in the mornings and Papa would often read us interesting little facts from the set of *Tell Me Whys* he'd got for us. Later in the morning, sitting under the shade of a huge deodar in his private lawn, Papa would teach us bits of history from one of his old school textbooks, and in the evenings, we would troop down behind him in single file in height order—just like little police cadets—to the Kalatop sanctuary, where he'd point to the trees and other flora with his stick, asking each of us in turn, the names of the trees and wild-flowers. These rambles included all the family children, whoever was up for the summer. Papa was quite strict with us and we dreaded the nature rambles and lessons in history.

One year Papa decided to bring a tutor up to Dalhousie so that we had a well-defined routine, with the mornings spent in learning. But this didn't work out the way Papa had planned. We took the tutor on a nature ramble, telling him we would show him all we knew, and as we progressed deeper into the Kalatop sanctuary, we drifted away one by one, till the last one of us left said he needed a loo break and disappeared as well. That poor tutor was left wandering the woods, completely lost. A search party was sent to look for him as darkness was descending—all the kids were home but no tutor. That unfortunate man's story hardly needs telling—obviously he left and we were punished.

During the winter, we would go for shikaars on weekends, mostly into the low hills and kikar forests of Ropar along the Satluj river where Papa's uncle, Sardar Sudarshan Singh, has a beautiful little fort on a hill. The whole family, including aunts, uncles, cousins, dogs, and beaters would go on camps he organized.

What a treat these shikaars were! We would hunt partridge, boar, and sometimes duck. Papa was very 'pukka' about only shooting what one could eat. Laws of shikaar, he would say. Once Virji and my cousin Girimer Vir shot down some crows. Papa was livid, threatening to have them cooked for the boys' dinner, and only when they turned green and looked abjectly cowed and apologetic did he relent.

Bharatgarh Fort was a grand holiday place for us children, with its meandering corridors and ghostly rooms. It had thunder boxes (dry latrines) on the roof, lit by a night lantern in an alcove, which one needed to carry up the steep stairs if one needed the potty at night. The fort was a haven of myriads of games. Of course, it has now all been changed into a rather posh, boutique resort.

After Faridkot, Papa was posted to Patiala as the assistant inspector general (AIG) of the Railways. It was good to be in Patiala, which was close to Chandigarh and our village, and we could visit Ammiji and Bapuji on weekends. Patiala was also bustling and lively compared to the one-horse towns, Ferozepur and Faridkot, we had lived in earlier.

As AIG, Papa travelled in a beautiful saloon, which was attached to any train in which he rode. We were taken along once. The saloon had a bedroom, bathroom, dining room, and a tiny drawing room attached. Papa tells me that an AIG who succeeded him abandoned this beautiful bogey in Lahore when he was invited for a meeting with his Pakistani counterpart just so that he could drive back across the border faster. I wonder if the poor saloon is still languishing in Lahore . . .

Our home in Patiala also, funnily, resembled a train. Drawing room, dining room, guestroom, our parents' room, followed by our room and a little room converted into a nursery for Nanki. Compartment to compartment, room to room. The large garden had a jamun tree on one side and huge eucalyptus trees in front, quarters at the back for the staff and a small annex.

I was enrolled in Yadavindra Public School (YPS), a school housed in a majestic building. The school was started by Maharaja Yadavindra Singh of Patiala and named after him. It was meant to replace Lahore's Aitchison College, now lost to us after Partition.

Our riding lessons continued at the police lines (colony), which were close to our house. When Virji was home on holiday we would ride every morning with our cousins.

The Patiala jail bordered the police riding school and often, we would clamber up the boundary wall to watch the shackled prisoners working in the jail fields. We would be fascinated to see real-life prisoners at close quarters. We were forbidden from speaking to the prisoners, but one of my cousins, not being able to resist striking up a conversation with a prisoner asked him, 'Qaidiji, why are you here?' Before he could answer we were spotted by one of the policemen on the riding school side of the wall and whisked away.

Papa remembers an incident from his time with the Railways in Patiala. A nihang, a warrior-saint, boarded an empty wagon of a goods train astride his horse. When a ticket collector asked him for his ticket, he replied that he didn't have one. When the official insisted that he buy one, the nihang answered, 'TC sahib, you will have to ask my horse to buy one since I'm on his back and not occupying a seat.' He was allowed to ride free.

An acquaintance from Fazilka had given Papa a huge beautiful fully grown St Bernard dog, much to Mama's dismay. Mama does not like dogs but has had to spend her life with them because Papa at any given time has to have at least two. The dog was called Vicky, named so by her previous owners. She was very excitable and quite impossible to control, often scaring visitors and sometimes throwing them to the floor by hurling herself at them in her excitement to greet them. She earned herself a reputation and soon no one came unannounced to visit us.

Mama enjoyed Patiala too, for her sister lived there. She also had a circle of rummy- and bridge-playing friends in the city. Nanki was a baby then and spent most of her time under the supervision of a stern old bai. She was often sick—she was born with weak lungs and pneumonia—and Mama often had to rush her off to Chandigarh for medical attention. I would be left behind and move to Moti Bagh palace, my masi's home.

I loved being with her, my uncle, and cousins. The gardens at Moti Bagh were large and offered innumerable treasures and games to be thought up. My cousin Jaya Bhen was great at thinking them up and Tikkoo Vir was very adept at disruption. Pavan Bhen was often with us as well and she taught me how to swim, which I learnt kicking and screeching, but I did learn.

During this time Papa was mostly away on tour. He would spend the odd evening with us, which we loved. His presence always added something special. Pavan Bhen and he would get into serious debates about life and religion, specially on the tenets of Sikhism, which Papa was so staunch about, but she, a good Sikh at heart, would seek to question. We were fascinated to see this side of Papa, which allowed the arguments and accepted Pavan's point of view. We cherished and enjoyed these rare moments.

Recently, we were having lunch together at Chhote Bhuaji's when Papa got up to take his spaniel pup out for a wee. I asked, 'Why don't you let one of the staff take Abu out, you're in the middle of your lunch?'

'He's my baby and I have to look after him,' Papa replied.

'I wish you'd done the same for us, you abandoned us for so many years,' I said pettily.

I saw my father's face fall and an uncomfortable silence

descended on the table. My bhua later chastised me for hurting my father with my unthinking remark. To her he would always be her selfless brother who sacrificed his job and years of his life upholding his beliefs, humanitarian and religious.

From Patiala, Papa was posted to Chandigarh again, as superintendent of police (SP), CID training. He was in charge of political and criminal intelligence and his duties further required him to train subordinate staff in collecting intelligence, carrying out surveillance of suspects, and censoring mail and telephone calls. Papa told his subordinates about the masterful escapades of the famous British spy Kim Philby who worked as a double agent before defecting to the Soviet Union. He also brought to their attention the fact one could always be seduced by women, giving the examples of Mata Hari and Christine Keeler's liaison with the British war minister. The intention was to bring home to his trainees that one's guard must always be up and one must always be wary of any such liaisons in the higher echelons of the bureaucracy, politics, military, and intelligence. Papa taught his trainees never to be scared by anyone's rank as far as security was concerned. They were also trained for capture and interrogation. The rule was to volunteer no information. In a sense, Papa was prepared for dealing with the future turn of events in his life.

Sadly, there is no school to teach families how to deal with the despair of a loved one being tortured. Several of his former police trainees told him how they had profited from his strict training. Little did he know in what good stead this would hold him.

My father's last posting before he resigned was to Bombay. He took over as group commandant of the Central Industrial Security Force (CISF) in the winter of 1982. Mama went with him first and stayed with relatives till he was allotted a flat on Nepean Sea Road, after which we joined them.

Nanki dressed in her first salwar-kameez in the balcony of our Bombay flat

We spent some of the best years of our life in Bombay. My mother, especially, loved being there. I think she had a sense of freedom there that she had never had before and hasn't had since. For three years we were happy as a family, even though Virji was away at boarding school most of the time.

Virji, Nanki and I in Bombay. Virji is in his nightsuit because he was down with jaundice and home from Welham. Nanki and I were busy with our dolls when we were asked to pose for this photo.

Bombay was very exciting. Emaan, Nanki, and I had never seen the sea before, or a double-decker bus for that matter. Our flat was sea-facing and overlooked a flyover, beyond which was a large expanse of rocks and then the sea, which stretched far into the horizon.

I was enrolled in Walsingham High, an all-girls' school down the road from where we lived. Nanki joined the kindergarten there a year later. Papa's office was on Dadabhai Naoroji Road in an old building with an ancient lift.

We would look forward to our rare visits to Papa's office. We would go up in the rickety old lift, which was like a cage, and would be greeted by Mr Kutty, Papa's secretary. Papa would order idlis for our lunch after which Ma, Nanki, and I would push off for home on a bus. When Virji was home from boarding school, we would sit together in the evenings and play card games with Papa,

Pa, Mama, Virji, Nanki and I in Bombay, shortly before Pa vanished.

one called court piece and the other bhabo. Virji was a bad loser and would often throw his cards in and go off in a huff, which would have us all in splits of laughter, annoying him further.

Some evenings, Papa and Mama would try and teach us how to waltz, with Strauss playing on our new music system. My parents love music, and had finally bought themselves a good system. Records were becoming obsolete and cassettes were all the rage. Papa bought me my first cassette; we walked down to a little cassette shop at the Nepean Sea Road market and I chose 'Disco Deewane' by Nazia Hasan.

'Are you sure this is the one you want?' Papa asked, quite horrified, I think, that I had not chosen something a little more dignified, perhaps Mozart or Beethoven.

Mama and Papa had joined a Western music appreciation class at the Max Müeller Bhavan, which they enjoyed immensely. The class was taught by Farah Rustam. Farah had been male before she underwent a sex change.

During one of their classes, when Farah was trying to push a heavy grand piano around, Papa jumped up and volunteered to help, exclaiming, 'How can I let a lady move such heavy equipment?' Then one day she said that for the next week or so they wouldn't see her as she would be in hospital having her breasts enlarged. Papa sent her a get-well-soon note. Farah took her class through all the great classical masters: Mozart, Debussy, Schumann. Curiously, one of the charges of sedition against my father, amongst the many others, was his taking Western classical music lessons, which was seen as anti-national.

On Fridays, Mama and Papa would dress up and go to the races to bet on horses. One Children's Day we were taken along. I placed my bet on a horse called Diana. There was much excitement.

'My horse will win, won't it, Papa?'

'I'm sure it will, darling,' he said.

The race started. Out came the thundering horses from their stalls. We leaned against the railing, cheering our own. It was so exhilarating! The race ended and, horrors of horrors! Diana finished last.

Papa and Mama off to the races in Bombay

I was crestfallen. To compensate, Papa got me an orange bar and all was well again.

We were members of the National Theatre of Performing Arts (NCPA) and my parents would never miss the chance to expose us to theatre, ballet, and dance recitals. We got to see *Evita*—with Sharon Prabhakar acting as Eva Peron and singing *Don't cry for me Argentina.* What a show that was! And the Bolshoi ballet performing *Swan Lake* transported me into a flight of fantasy with me as a ballerina.

My father's cousin Janak Chachaji came to live with us in 1983. We had one spare bedroom in the flat and that became his room. He loved music too, especially the Moody Blues and Fleetwood Mac. I still remember 'Sitting at the wheel', by the Moody Blues, blaring on the system.

Me aged 10 in Bombay

Me in Bombay

It was nice having Janak Chachaji live with us. While he was with us, he got married and his wife Preneet Chachiji came to stay with us too. At first Virji and I were a little put out with her arrival because it meant sharing Janak Chachaji's time and affection with another person but she soon won us over and we were quite happy to have her around as well.

These were the 'wonder years' of togetherness before the storm hit our home.

5

Punjab, pre-partition

EARLY ONE MORNING, not so long ago, a Sardar galloped across his lands, a blur of white across the green landscape, with his zaildar, the irrigation manager of the local area, and his stable manager trying to keep pace. He was running late—the train at Narangwal station had been stopped and was waiting to ferry him to Shahdara, where he would hold court. All around, as far as the eye could see, were his lands.

As he approached the tiny sleepy station, he slowed his horse to a canter and rode right up to the train, dismounted and jumped aboard his next ride. He slipped into a black achkaan handed to him by Kartar Singh, the zaildar, and then raised his hand, gesturing for the train to get a move on. As the train slowly chugged out of the station, my grandfather, Sardar Bahadur Joginder Singh Mann, MBE (Member of the British Empire), Hon.

First Class Magistrate, stretched out his legs and fell asleep.

He had gone to his village for the weekend to check on accounts and his lands, staying at the rather uncomfortable mud fort his father had built. His three mothers lived there, each within her own set of rooms and courtyards. The haveli at Qila Sardar Harnam Singh was built on a large rectangular plot of land, with the village surrounding it. The entrance was through a big deori or gateway, with a gurdwara on one side and a guesthouse on the other. Beyond this deori were the quarters, kitchens, stables, cowsheds and, further in, rooms for my great-grandfather's first two wives and their families. Upstairs were two burjs (tower rooms), one kept locked and opened only for my grandmother's rare visits, and one where my great-grandfather's favourite wife Maaji Rani Sahib lived. Outside the walls of the fort my great-grandfather had a school, hospital, veterinary hospital, a post office, and a bank built for the village.

My great-grandfather's second wife was my grandfather's (Bapuji's) mother. My great-grandfather married his first wife's younger sister after his first wife failed to produce any children, and from this union was born my grandfather. So the first and second maajis lived happily in their village home, sharing a son and an heir.

My great-grandfather Sardar Harnam Singh then fell in love with the third maaji or Maaji Rani Sahib, as she was called, and married her. Legend has it that he abducted her from her parents' home and carried her off to his home on horseback. Maaji's parents weren't too distressed as Wade Bapuji was very wealthy and a bigger sardari than themselves. My great-grandfather and Maaji Rani Sahib had another son, who died, and a daughter, half-sister to my grandfather.

Back to my snoozing grandfather on the train to Shahdara: feeling the train slow down, he woke up, instantly alert, and quickly changed from his travel-worn breeches and riding boots into a smart suit stitched by Rankins of Lahore. Dapper now, my bowlegged Bapuji stepped out into the hustle of Shahdara station, and into his waiting Buick and was driven to court where he would be judge for the rest of the day.

In the summer months, my great-grandfather would take off for Pahalgam and Srinagar with his favourite wife, her mother, his son and daughter and a whole retinue of staff, leaving behind his first two wives, or sarkaars, as they were called, to look after his home. They would travel in buggies for days together, stopping only for the nights at resthouses along the way. Escaping the scorching heat of the plains, they would be guests of the Maharaja of Kashmir in Srinagar.

Legend has it that the Mann Sardars, my father's progenitors, were a Rajput tribe from the deserts of Jaisalmer. They had migrated north, settling in the fertile plains of the Punjab on the banks of the Ravi river, and over generations accumulated vast tracts of land, eventually becoming feudal landlords. Even though my great-grandfather got the short end of the stick, inheriting barren land, he worked hard and with some help from the British, who dug out a canal from the Chenab river just so his lands could be irrigated, my great-grandfather handed over a very rich legacy of around seven thousand acres and seven villages to my grandfather, along with various honorary titles bestowed by the British and passed on from father to son. According to *Chiefs and Families of Note in the Punjab* by Lepel H. Griffin and Charles Francis Massy, 'The Punjab proverb says, "The Mann Sardars are gallant, handsome and true"'; and Budh Singh upheld the fame of his house and stayed true to the British. He was idolized by the army and remained faithful to the end. On the return of peace his jagirs, amounting to 6340 were confirmed to him for life and Rs 1040 was released to his male heirs in perpetuity. His grandson Harnam Singh, my great-grandfather, an honorary magistrate in Mananwala.

In pre-Partition India, all the chiefs studied at Aitchison College, Lahore, and Sardar Harnam Singh was also sent there with an entourage of staff, syces, and horses. He didn't enjoy the disciplined life of school and after a short

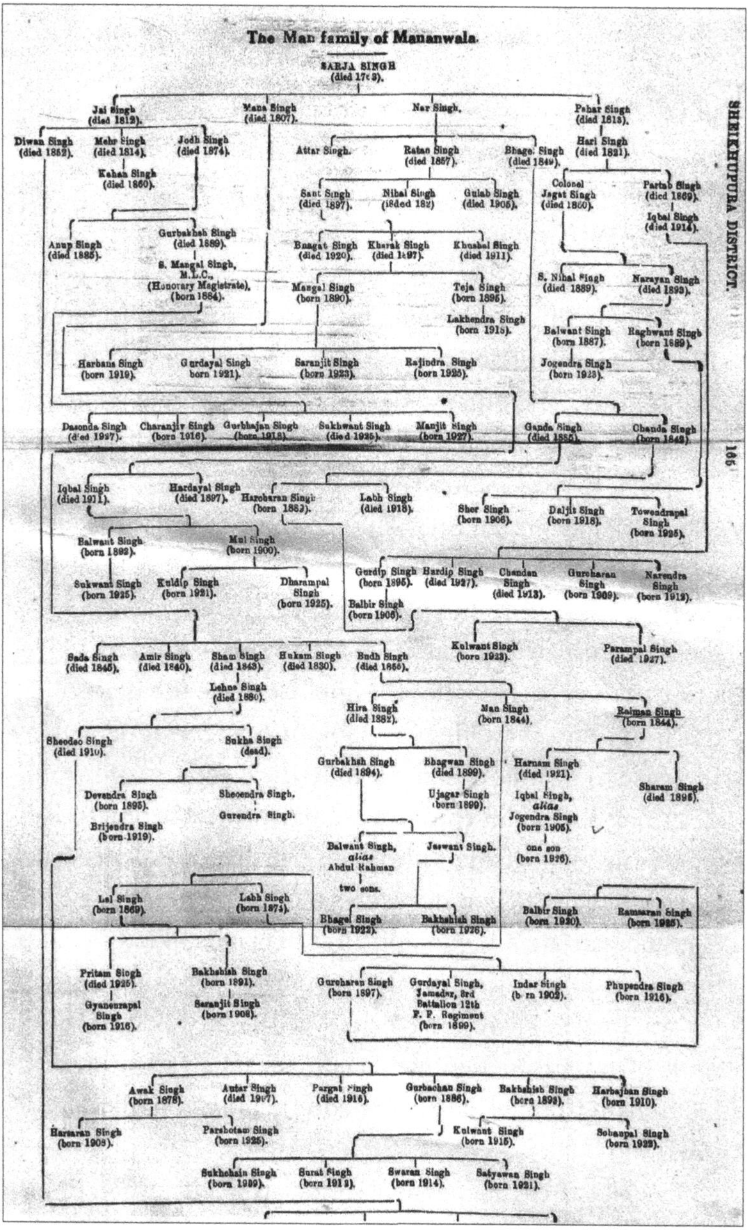

Our family tree

stint decided to leave Chiefs College and return home to his lands, where he built a mud fort for his family and named it after himself. Our village in Punjab today is called Qila Sardar Harnam Singh in his memory.

The sardars of the time supported the Raj and were given many titles and shown favour for services rendered. The titles Sardar Bahadur and MBE were conferred on my grandfather. My father's maternal grandparents were Sir and Lady Arur Singh. Sir Arur Singh was the honorary caretaker of the Golden Temple.

Bapuji, my grandfather, studied at Aitchison College as well and won the coveted Rewaz Medal, a solid gold medal given for best all-round performance. He was elected into the first Punjab Legislative Assembly in Lahore in 1937. Prior to that, in 1935, he was appointed by the British to the India Reserve Office as captain for recruitment. He resigned in 1937 as a major, fought the elections and won, defeating the Akali candidate, barrister Avtar Singh. He was a member of the Shiromani Gurdwara Prabandhak Committee (SGPC) and, besides being an honorary first-class magistrate and looking after his lands, Bapuji made his career in politics. He later became a recruiting officer for the British army for World War II and was given the rank of honorary lieutenant colonel. His full title was Lieutenant Colonel Sardar Bahadur Joginder Singh Mann, MBE.

In 1947, after Independence, he was made president of

the Rehabilitation Board. In 1949, he became the minister of revenue and rehabilitation. In 1952, he became a Member of Parliament in the Rajya Sabha as an Akali from Patiala and the East Punjab States Union (PEPSU). He fought the Akali Dal (Master Tara Singh) in 1967 and won, becoming speaker of the Punjab Assembly, which was dissolved by him in 1968 because Laxman Singh Gill's government, supported by the Congress, had lost its majority and there was pandemonium.

Bapuji and Amiji, pre-Partition in Lahore

My grandfather married my grandmother when he was twenty-one years old. At the time she was a child of eleven and the only daughter of Sir Arur Singh.

My grandmother, Ammiji, went to her marital home at the age of thirteen, along with a huge trousseau of gold, silver, jewels, clothes, and dolls! She would tell us stories about the early days of her marriage, three mothers-in-law, purdah parties and life in the mud fort, her town house in Shahdara, and games of dolls played with her mothers-in-law. Ammiji was thoroughly spoilt and coddled and lived an easy life. My Bapuji would carry on with his political and magisterial affairs while pandering to his wife's every whim and fancy.

Ammiji told us of how there would always be a darzi sitting at home conjuring up one exquisite outfit after another for her. She was very well-dressed and would never repeat an outfit when she went out. Sometimes the poor tailor master would sit up all night sewing so that Ammiji would have a new ghagra, a long flowing skirt, for the next day. In those days my grandmother and her contemporaries wore ghagras with borders of real silver or gold work. To give the outfit weight and make it fall better, she would sometimes have gold coins sewn into the hem. At home, she would wear kurtas with taang pyjamas but if she went shopping or to call on someone, she would slip into one of these voluminous ghagras, cover her head with a dupatta on top of which she would drape another long piece of cloth called a chadar, which would completely hide her form in observance of the strict purdah.

We would listen to Ammiji's stories goggle-eyed. They sounded as if they were straight out of a fairytale. She would tell us an anecdote or two and one could see the joy light up her usually sad and closed face. Then she would suddenly stop and we would beg for more. 'One more story of the old days, Ammiji, just one more,' Bhavani Bhen and I would beg.

'Nai, bas, no more . . . those days are long gone. It was another world,' she'd say, lowering her sunglasses back down over her eyes so one couldn't look in. In her way she was pulling the shutters down on her bygone, better life.

Ammiji had also travelled extensively, accompanying my grandfather around the world. But although she could read and write and knew a great deal of Sikh history and the scriptures, one of her biggest regrets was that she had had no formal education.

Ammiji recounted how on one trip, when they were in Venice enjoying a gondola ride with a French couple, the lady tried to strike up a conversation with Ammiji but all she could understand was '*Parlez vous Francais*?' She would break out into gales of laughter whenever she told us about this little incident.

My grandparents had six children, two of whom died of diphtheria. My uncle Manjit Singh, the eldest, was born in 1929 and followed the family tradition by studying at

Aitchison College. He was among the first Sikh boys to study at Oxford. He read at Exeter College, where his philosophy teacher was Dr Sarvapelli Radhakrishnan. Zulfikar Ali Bhutto was his classmate.

My aunts, Inderjit Kaur and Daljit Kaur, born after him, studied at Queen Mary's in Lahore and after Partition at Chelsea and St Bede's in Simla. Ammiji had plans to send her daughters to a Swiss finishing school, but the Partition in 1947 and the loss of their properties and wealth ended her dream. She, however, still made sure her children had the best possible education available in those days, ensuring that they never felt the lack of an education as she had.

Papa, the youngest of Bapuji and Ammiji's children, was born on 20 May 1945 in Simla at their home 'Bohemia', which is close to my maternal grandparents' summer home. Around this time rumbles of Partition had begun to be felt and Simla, being the epicentre because it was the summer capital of the British government, got all the news. Nobody believed that Punjab would actually be partitioned. My grandfather, who was actively involved in politics, felt, along with many other educated and influential Sikhs, that if the Hindus and Muslims could have their own countries, why not the Sikhs?

In hindsight, the seeds for the idea of a separate state were sown in my father's mind at an early age and nurtured by his mother, a staunch Sikh and a great motivational force for him.

My family was already in Simla for the summer during the throes of Partition. Although they suffered no casualties and lost none of their immediate family, they were affected in that their lands, homes, and belongings were all left behind in Pakistan. As the reality sank in along with the realization of what they had lost in terms of wealth, land, and social standing, they grew progressively disillusioned by the idea of Partition, particularly given what the Sikhs went through and the losses they themselves suffered.

My father recollects a Muslim manservant, Hussain, a playmate of his who had come up to Simla along with the family for the summer. At Partition, Hussain was left on the Indian side with my family in Simla. My grandmother cleverly gave Hussain a Hindu name, lest his life was endangered. But my father, not entirely understanding the danger, could never remember to call Hussain by his Hindu name and would get sharply reprimanded by Amiji who feared for Hussain's life and safety.

Hussain was later escorted to the Wagah border, near Amritsar, much to the dismay of my father, so he could be reunited with his own family in the newly created Pakistan.

After Partition, my grandfather was allotted a village

called Wazir Khera, near Kaithal in present-day Haryana, in lieu of his land in Pakistan. The Muslim landlord who owned this village had to leave for Pakistan, just as my grandparents had to leave all their land and belongings across the newly formed border.

The house my grandparents inherited with the land was not what they had been accustomed to, but they never looked back. They started the process of settling in to a much-altered life minus the comforts that had been part of their day-to-day lives.

The 'haveli' they got had a mud floor that had to be freshly coated with cow dung every week. One day, while a worker was fetching hay from a haystack for the cattle feed, his pitchfork hit something metallic with a loud clang. He dug deeper and found a Studebaker car hidden away under the hay, probably by the Muslims who had lived there and had had to flee. They must have hidden the car to save it from looters and in the hope that they would be back soon. No one knows what became of the family that had to cross over, but this brand new Studebaker—it had only done a few miles—became one of the family's most precious finds and must have provided some respite in those grim days.

Eventually Bapuji, on the invitation of Maharaja Yadavindra Singh, a close friend of his, shifted base to Sirhind in the princely state of Patiala, and built his house on his own land.

6

AS A CHILD, Papa was fascinated with uniforms and persuaded his mother to get various military outfits for him, which he would wear and parade around in, prompting the family to refer to him affectionately as 'Major Sahib'. Once, walking down the Mall in Simla in the full regalia of a major—he must have been about six years old—with his mother and sisters, he threw a tantrum, kicking and screaming because Amiji wouldn't buy him a dinky car. Along came a real live army officer and said, 'Behave yourself, Major, you're in uniform!' which stopped Papa mid-wail much to the relief of Amiji who thanked the officer and marched her son home.

My father started his school days in Simla at the Convent of Jesus and Mary, an all-girls' school, where his sisters studied. He was taken in as a special favour and, being the only boy, was thoroughly spoilt by the nuns and students. He later went to Bishop Cotton School, a boarding school, also in Simla.

Bapuji and Amiji (seated); standing left to right Tayaji, Pa, Wade Buaji and Chhote Buaji—Pa in his favourite Major Saab uniform with his parents and siblings just after Partition.

Pa in the hockey team at Bishop Cotton School Simla. (standing centre with glasses)

At Bishop Cotton School, he was a fairly good student, excelling in history and English, in which he won the Hailey Prize for Literature and the Shakespeare Prize in his final year. He often tells us about his time at the school and the antics he and his friends would get up to. One story is about passing a boy a leaf of bichhu buti, stinging nettle, when the boy was sitting on the pot, rather than his carefully rationed six squares of toilet paper a day.

After finishing school, Papa joined the Government College in Chandigarh. His parents had refused to send him to either Oxford, like his brother, or to St Stephens, fearing he would be led astray (like his older brother, who had the time of his life during his Oxford years, playing the playboy across Europe) so he stayed close to home. He studied his favourite subject, history, and did extremely well, graduating with a gold medal in History Honours.

Immediately after college, he began preparing for the All India Services exam. He did brilliantly, clearing all the exams, including the one for the Indian Foreign Service, but chose to join the Indian Police Service (IPS), finally realizing his dream of being an officer in uniform. His ranking was very high and he was assigned to his home cadre of Punjab.

Papa was sent to Mussoorie for training. When his fellow officers in training asked him where he was from my father, being facetious, blithely replied, 'Scotland Yard', earning him the sobriquet Scotty.

Papa in Mussoorie for his officers' training (standing last row centre)

The drill officer at the training centre, a Mr Burge, had a soft corner for boys from public schools and Papa quickly became one of his favourites. He was chosen by Mr Burge to lead the passing out parade, which would have been all very well but my father, tall and lanky, walks . . . how should I describe it . . . sort of like a camel, not exactly with the gait of an impressive marching leader. Just before the final parade, as luck would have it, Mr Burge was transferred and replaced by a Mr Rathore, who was shocked to see such an ungainly leader of the marchpast.

He promptly replaced Papa and sent him to the end of the formation.

My father started his police career as an assistant superintendent police posted in Ludhiana. In 1970 he married my mother, Geetinder Kaur (Geeta), daughter of Indian Civil Service (ICS) officer Sardar Gyan Singh Kahlon. Mama was twenty-one when they married. The wedding was a happy affair in Simla, where my father obliged his sisters-in-law by doing cartwheels rather than singing, as demanded by Mama's cousins. He very proudly tells us that he did a neat cartwheel into Mama's heart without his turban coming off, much to the amazement of his gaping sisters-in-law.

Early cop days

Pa on posting as ADC to the Governor of Punjab

Papa in Jaisalmer on police training

Mama had graduated from St Bede's College, as did my bhuas and masi. She has two siblings, an older sister Preneet Kaur, married to the Maharaja of Patiala, and who was the minister of state for external affairs in the second Manmohan Singh government, and her younger brother Himmat Singh, retired from the United Nations. The three spent most of their childhood in Simla (much like Papa) and were brought up amongst a large extended family of aunts, uncles, and cousins. They had an idyllic childhood with memories of a simple, sheltered, and well-ordered life. Nanaji, my maternal grandfather, was a stickler for etiquette and rules and, much influenced by the English

Mama at a debate in St. Bede's College, Simla

and his college days at Oxford, lived the life of an English gentleman.

After my parents married, they set up house in Chandigarh, my father as the ADC to the governor of Punjab, Dr D.C. Pavate, and my mother looking after the

Pa and Mama at their wedding in 1970

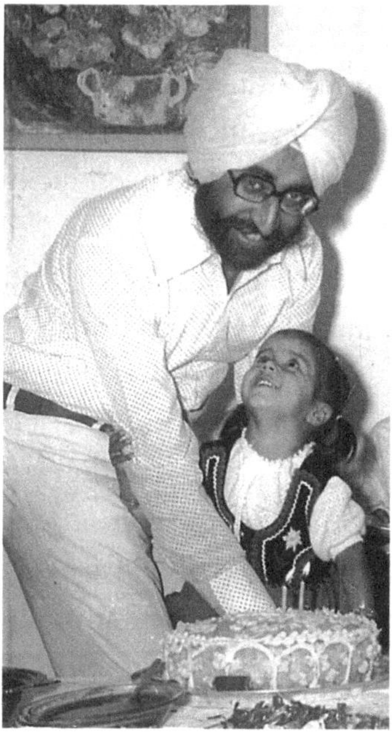

Me looking up devotedly at Pa on my second birthday

home. Virji, my elder brother, arrived within a year of their marriage.

My father acquired a reputation for being a straightforward and honest officer. Once when Dr Pavate was out for a walk with only Papa for company, someone asked him if he felt scared walking without an escort. He promptly replied, 'Scared! With Mr Mann by my side, I need fear nothing.' Throughout his career in the police, he commanded tremendous respect, even fear, for he was a strict disciplinarian.

In 1972, when my brother was about ten months old, my parents left him in the care of my aunt and went off on their first trip to England and the Continent. They were very excited because they had been lucky enough to get passes for the Munich Olympics.

The tragedy at the Olympic Village, where the members of the Israeli team were gunned down, deeply saddened my father and as a sign of protest, my parents left. My father abhors violence of any kind.

Recently, Papa and I sat together after dinner and watched Steven Spielberg's *Munich*, a movie about the 1972 Olympic massacre. The next morning Papa said to me, 'Darling, weren't you scared at night after watching such a violent movie? I had nightmares all night.'

I often wonder what went wrong—how did this gentle father of mine get himself behind bars?

When Mama and Papa returned to India after their travels in Europe, Emaan didn't recognize them. A year later, in October 1973, I was born.

When I was just six weeks old, Papa had to go to Mount Abu for his Senior Officers' Training. We left for Mount Abu in Papa's Fiat car, with Papa at the wheel, and Ma, Virji, I, the bai, one staff, and Tipu, the German alsatian, packed in the back seat like sardines.

Once his course was over, he was posted to Jullundur (now Jalandhar), Ferozepur, and Chandigarh in the Vigilance department and then back to Ferozepur as SSP.

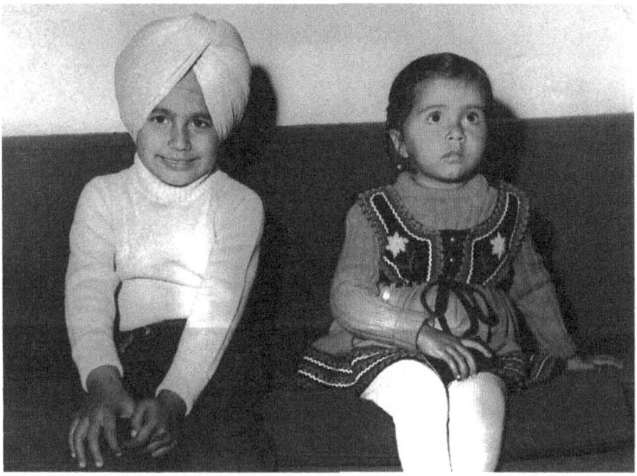

Virji and I, aged 4 and 2

Pa, Mama, Virji and I at a party at Chhote Buaji house in 1975

7

BACK HOME IN Chandigarh, trying to come to terms with the fact that my father was in prison for God alone knew how long, we were all thrown unwillingly into the spotlight. It was difficult to cope, more so for my brother who was in boarding school. He asked to be brought home and joined us in our henhouse. My boisterous brother had withdrawn into his own little world of books and his pet Alsatian, Cleo.

Nanki in Chandigarh with Cleo

The first time I visited my father in jail was in the summer of 1985 in Bharatpur. I had been longing to meet him but I had no idea what to expect as we had not been told about the torture he had endured. Virji, Nanki, and I, along with Mama, my grandparents, and Chhote Bhuaji drove to Bharatpur. It was a long, hot journey in a trusty Ambassador car with a broken air-conditioner. Finally, we arrived at the large yellow building of the Sewar Jail in Bharatpur. I felt like I had been transported into the movies—the only place I had ever seen a prison before, other than the Patiala jail years ago, which shared a boundary wall with the police riding school and where we had tried to strike up conversations with the shackled prisoners on the sly. It all seemed so surreal!

We waited in the sweltering heat in the car, fanning ourselves with newspapers and magazines for two hours. The three of us, Virji, Nanki, and I, were growing more impatient by the minute. We were finally led into the prison, after being frisked and searched, first through the big iron doors, then into a little courtyard that had the jail superintendent's office on one side. It was a dingy, cold room with jail officials and policemen in plainclothes standing around. Behind the chair on which I sat was a little barred window that opened into the inner compound of the prison—I tried to imagine my father somewhere in there with all kinds of criminals.

After a while, Papa walked in through the door from which we had entered. Only we had come in from outside, free, and he from a cell, captive. He walked in, smiling, and everyone rose. I smiled back at him. He looked at me and said, 'Oh Pitsy, you are here to see me, darling?'

I nodded my head, holding back tears, and hugged him, unable to speak. One could see he had suffered though he was trying hard to camouflage it by smiling at all of us. Nanki and I sat on his lap, but I can't remember where Emaan was. Mama was on the chair next to Papa.

Papa looked at me and said, 'Pitsy, do you know this room is bugged?'

One of the policemen sitting nearby heard and exclaimed loudly 'Nahin, nahin, Mann Sahib, it is not bugged.'

We all laughed. Later, we learnt from our lawyer that the room was indeed bugged. As time went by we would get used to the indignity of being frisked, of being surrounded by armies of policemen who overheard our conversations, of letters being opened and tampered with, of phones being tapped and of the general surveillance. My father whispered to me, 'I hope you are being strong, studying hard and saying your prayers?'

Once again I nodded a silent yes. I knew if I spoke I would cry.

The forty-five minutes allowed us were up and my father was all too soon led back into his cell. We were escorted

Pa produced in court during his trial getting a few minutes with Mama. In Bhagalpur

out, the sun was still shining bright as ever, the birds were noisy, but we were all quiet, lost in our own thoughts.

Months became years and still no one could see the light at the end of the long, dark tunnel. In the course of the year we children visited my father turn by turn so that every few months he got to see one of us. In all those years I must have met my father four or five times through a tiny barred window, forty-five minutes at a time.

The memory of his birthday has stayed with me. Every year, Mama or Ammiji would tell us to make a card or write a birthday letter for Papa. I never did so because what would I write? 'Have a happy day and a wonderful year'? It would have been too cruel to make him a birthday card, I felt. Nonetheless I would make a card and write in it, but would end up shredding it to bits, year after year.

After Papa was shifted to the Bhagalpur jail in Bihar, we went on a futile attempt to meet him on his birthday the following year, in May 1986. We were not given permission and had to return, dejected, to our pokey little hotel room in Bhagalpur to see him the next morning in court. He was shifted to Bhagalpur because the government wanted to detain him longer—he had won the NSA case slapped on him, the reason for his being in Bharatpur, so the government had to shift him out of Rajasthan to keep him in jail longer.

The government now charged Papa with sedition. Before being brought to Bhagalpur, Papa had been taken to Bombay for a case registered against him for an interview he'd given Shobhaa De for *Celebrity* magazine just after he'd resigned from his police job. In Bombay, he was kept imprisoned at a police station for the duration of his questioning, and without legal aid. The small cell in which he was housed was filthy and the thin mattress provided to him was full of fleas.

8

The judge banged down hard on the table with his gavel.

'Order!,' he shouted repeatedly.

My father had just been led in, heavily shackled and manacled, and the clanking of chains could be heard by all in the courtroom. Noise and confusion resulted as everyone jostled to get a glimpse of him coming through the door.

I sat on a chair facing the judge. There was a policewoman on either side of me. I stood up to catch a glimpse of my father but was quickly yanked back into my chair. The proceedings had begun; the police were late in producing my father.

When Papa saw Nanki, he picked her up and held her close but the judge told him to put her down. Papa complied but one could tell he was very hurt. He craved to hold his children close but was never allowed. He often mentions his desire to be with us, his children, and of missing out on our growing years in his diary entries.

Eleven months had passed since I had seen Papa. I was both excited and apprehensive about seeing him again—

there was much I wanted to tell him but I was not sure he would now understand.

Three years had passed since his imprisonment; we were young children when he was first arrested, now Virji and I were teenagers. Here he was in shackles, standing in an accused man's dock, on trial for heinous crimes like conspiracy to assassinate the late prime minister and waging war against the country.

As the trial proceeded, witnesses were produced, and one by one Mr Roy, Mr Vadhera and later, Mr Ram Jethmalani, Papa's lawyers, proved their testimonies to be false. If it hadn't been our father's life in question, it would have been rather a laugh.

There was the incident of the cook, who was produced as a government witness, shaking and trembling. He testified that he had been the family cook for three or four years, and had seen various people come to our house at specific times and on specific dates to visit. He remembered all the dates and the names of the visitors but when cross-examined, he could not remember the children's names. He eventually broke down and admitted to being tutored.

I remember being in shock watching Rewat Singh, our cook, cooking up stories. It was a nightmarish trip to Bhagalpur for me. When the court proceedings finally ended, Pa was immediately surrounded by police to be led away. I ran towards him, shocked that he was going to be senior officer (Mann resigned from the post of Deputy Inspector General, CISF), how can they handcuff him? Where there are 10 men to guard him, they can put 10 more," said one IG.

But that's not all. Pavit Kaur, who has visited Mann before and is therefore right in saying that the jail authorities know her, walked down with Mann till the waiting van ("Better wash your hair today," he advised her), surrounded by cops. But she was content in the knowledge that she'd meet him alone (ie, with bars between them—nobody can meet him without these—and cops seated in a corner of the room) the next day.

Her eight-year-old sister however, whose letters to her father sometimes end with little drawings, never knows if he gets to read them. The drawings, says Mann's elder sister, Daljit Kaur, are seen by Mann's jailors as escape plans. Similarly Salim Ali's book on birds, and the *William* series of books have been withheld. Punjabi books are withheld because apparently nobody in Bhagalpur Jail can read Punjabi and censor them. So are *rakhis* sent by Daljit—"Who knows what exactly the *rakhi* packet may contain?" shrugged an SP in Bihar.

Simranjit Singh Mann, 42, now president of the United Akali Dal, was arrested in Jogmani, Bihar, with four other Sikhs on November 29, 1984 as they were trying to cross the border to Nepal, in what seems too incredible a blunder for such an intelligent man. That stretch of the border is reportedly so narrow that all the security agencies have their posts on the same road. The Sikhs couldn't explain why they were going to Nepal: to add to it, the police had Mann's picture with them (he had gone underground soon after his resignation after Operation Bluestar in June 1984), and as the last straw, one of the five allegedly offered the cops a bribe of Rs lawyers alone. The notes made by his lawyer have to be shown

SS Mann: 'barriers of fear'

to the jail authorities.

Leading the team of lawyers fighting for him are Supreme Court counsels Ram Jethmalani, Dr B L Wadehra and 80-year-old Vinay Bhushan Rai, the seniormost member of the Bhagalpur Bar Association, who took the case despite strong opposition from his colleagues in the bar. On the other side, leading a team of five special public prosecutors, is Basudev Prasad, Patna's leading lawyer, who travels to and from Bhagalpur in a State aircraft, and who had initially argued the bail petitions for Mann's fellow accused in Patna!

The trial is already a year old, and likely to take another year, if the defence calls upon its own witnesses, despite the Special Judge having been appointed to exclusively hear this case. From about 102, 45 witnesses have been examined.

The charges against Mann in this case are 1) sedition (conspiracy to wage war against the State), 2) spreading disaffection between Hindus and Sikhs and 3) attempting to bribe a police officer. The main evidence available for the first two charges is documentary: the papers allegedly found on Mann when he was arrested, and the sure, presumably to prevent the journalists present (called as witnesses by the State) from talking to him. But Mann had them removed, appealing to the judge to remove this "barrier of fear between us and you in a free court". Though the police saw to it that the journalists didn't get at him for more than two minutes, this was enough for him to show them his yanked nailless toe and his plucked beard, as he got into the van.

Mann's relatives and lawyers see him as the key figure to a Punjab solution. They are convinced that he is the only one whom the militants (except the State-sponsored groups) will obey, not despite his absence from the scene for more than four years, but because of it—he is seen as the only one not to have compromised for power. The Centre has sent feelers, but Mann is supposed to have refused to talk to anyone but an official spokesman. Nor is he willing to give anything in writing, knowing that the person who strikes a deal with the Centre is doomed.

"If he's released without any preconditions, and allowed to travel around Punjab, meeting not only the militants but the people, we are sure he will bring peace to the State," says Daljit Kaur, his sister. But won't that itself be seen as a deal with the Centre? "No, because he will not accept any position, that would be the kiss of death for him." How will he face the opposition from State-sponsored groups, and those opposed to any Punjab solution? "They will be few, and won't last long," she says.

All that Mann would say on August 1 was "No solution in Punjab can be possible without the UAD", and "I have not approved of any committee" (referring to the UAD committee set up by Amarinder Singh last month). Five days later, his own committee had been announced.

State vs SS Mann

SPOTLIGHT

Jyoti Punwani attended the trial of the UAD leader in Bhagalpur court

"SIR, I am the 14-year old daughter of Sardar Simranjeet Singh Mann who is detained in Bihar at Bhagalpur. Due to my education and the distance between Chandigarh and Bihar, I went to meet my father on the 2nd of August after 11 months and in the excitement I forgot to take my Identity Card and of course the authorities knew who I was but they didn't let me see my father at all in the jail. Very upset, Pavit Kaur Mann, Chandigarh." (Letter to the editor, *The Indian Post*, received today.)

Pavit Kaur however, did get to see her father on August 1 as he was brought from Bhagalpur Central Jail to the Court of H K Verma, Special Judge, Bhagalpur, where Special Case 6/86, State Vs SS Mann and four others, is being heard since June '86. Brought there in a bus full of armed policemen, preceded and followed by security jeeps, he was not allowed to get down till the security men took their posts outside the court. When he finally alighted, he was the last of the five to do so, handcuffed, his legs tied to the same rope that bound them all. The fetters were removed in court.

Senior policemen close their eyes when they hear about the handcuffs and ropes. "Such a senior officer (Mann resigned from the post of Deputy Inspec-

62,000. With their luck, the cop refused. (Laughed the SP,"One takes bribes only according to one's capacity.")

Since then, Mann has been in jail. The Punjab government immediately charged him under the National Security Act, and he was lodged in Bharatpur Jail, Rajasthan, where, he says, his beard and toenails were yanked out, his private parts tortured. A petition by his wife says that he was not allowed to wear a turban. After that case, came the Bihar government's case. The Patna High Court ordered him to be lodged in Bhagalpur for security reasons.

In Bhagalpur he has not been physically tortured, except for an ulcer in his teeth not being attended to. He is in solitary confinement (the police ascribe this to his being given special prisoner status, asked for by him) and cannot meet even his lawyers alone. The notes made by his lawyer have to be shown

interviews given by him after he resigned.

Soon after Mann's arrest, a small news item appeared claiming that the CBI had found Mann involved in the conspiracy to kill Mrs Gandhi. Balbir Singh, who was acquitted last week of this charge, has claimed that he was asked to identify Mann and name him as one of the conspirators. Similar pressure is known to have been put upon some Sikhs in Bombay who are suspected of having attended a meeting allegedly addressed by Mann in Koliwada after his resignation. But no such charge has formally been made against him.

Surprisingly, the trial is being heard in an open court, not in jail. Apparently Ram Jethmalani's arguments against the Indira Gandhi assassination case being conducted in Tihar Jail influenced the decision to hold Mann's trial in what is commonly referred to as a "free court". Free it is. Despite the hundreds of policemen outside and inside it, Mann's relatives can talk to him in relative privacy, he in the accused's dock, they outside, when the court breaks for lunch.

On August 1, a row of policemen stood along the entire length of the accused's enclosure, presumably to prevent the journalists present (called as witnesses by the State) from

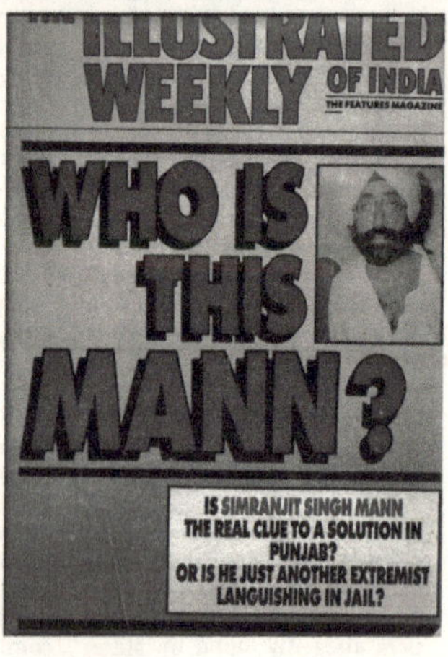

taken away so soon. Grabbing his shackled hand tightly, I walked down the stairs of the court house with him.

Seeing my distress Pa kept saying 'Be brave, be brave' to me. I was on the verge of tears.

'Papa', I said tremulously, 'don't leave me please,' even as the security was trying to pry me away from him.

He kissed me on my head and, hugging me tightly said, 'Baby you should wash your hair'—his way of trying to lighten the moment for my sake.

Before I could reply he quickly got on to the prison bus and left.

After these trips we would return, emotionally stripped, to Chandigarh and try to carry on with our lives as normally as possible.

The Japji Sahib mool mantra is a prayer every Sikh is supposed to recite first thing in the morning.

> There is One God,
> Whose name is Truth,
> The Creator,
> Without fear,
> Without hatred,
> Timeless in form,
> Beyond birth,
> Self-existent,
> Known by the Grace of the Guru.

I would wake up in our little bedroom in Chandigarh, and quickly recite this verse five times. Before sleeping, my last words would be the litany, which we had learned to recite as we learnt to speak. Only now there was a twist—I had made a pact with God: the mool mantra five times, one ardas at night and thirty-three chants of 'Waheguru' before I slept. No more, no less. I was obsessed with this ritual, and clung to it with absolute faith, thinking that if I kept my part of this little private bargain with God, He would surely, surely, send my father back home. I would add, 'Please bring my Papa home, I know You will,' besides a few other selfish requests: 'Please God, when I wake up in the morning may my face be clear of zits. Please, please.'

Mama in Simla, playing bridge with her family, a respite from her life of courtrooms and prison during Pa's imprisonment.

Being a teenager wasn't easy, especially with a father locked away in prison hundreds of kilometres away.

The new history teacher, a not-so-tall sardar with a beautifully tied turban, walked into the class with a flourish. He introduced himself and asked every child to stand up in turn and state his or her name and father's profession. The moment he said this, my hands got clammy, my legs started to tremble and I felt as if I would faint. God, let the ground swallow me! How can this man ask such personal questions?

The class didn't end before my turn and there was no gaping hole in the ground to swallow me up.

My turn came. I stood up.

Chhote Buaji and Nani at a dinner while Pa was in prison

Mama with her brood at the same dinner just before Papa was released

Virji and Girimer Vir in Chandigarh shortly before Pa's release in 1989

'Sir,' I said. 'My name is Pavit Kaur Mann and my father is a farmer.'

There, I'd told the lie. It was no one's business that my father was a political prisoner and not a farmer ploughing a field.

I was about to sit down, when the teacher said, 'Pavit Kaur Mann, are you sure that's what your father does?'

All of Class 7 was now staring at me.

I took a deep breath and something inside me snapped. I wasn't trembling any longer.

'No, sir, my father is in prison. He was a police officer. His name is Simranjit Singh Mann.'

I'd said it.

I stood straight and tall, meeting the teacher's eye, daring him silently to say something mean.

Instead, he said, 'Well done, Pavit. I'm glad you decided to tell the truth. You see all of us Sikhs are extremely proud of your father and you're a lucky girl to be his daughter.'

So that was that. Anyone who didn't know now knew.

A brief history of the sikhs

In order to understand the demand for a separate homeland, a brief look at the history of the Sikhs would be helpful.

W.H. McLeod in his *Historical Dictionary of Sikhism* states,

> For Sikhs, history and religion are inextricably intertwined. It is quite impossible to study the religion of the Sikhs without reference to their history. Likewise it is impossible to study the history without frequent recourse to their religion. The religion was born in historical events and it evolves in intimate response to the unfolding pattern of those events. To some extent this can be said of any religion. It is abundantly true of Sikhism.

In the middle ages there existed a void in the Indian subcontinent, created by Islam's bigotry and the rituals and caste system of Hinduism. Both scriptures were tough to follow—the Islamic scriptures were in Arabic and the Hindu in Sanskrit, making them inaccessible to the common man.

In the fifteenth century, Guru Nanak rejected the old order, creating a new religion. Sikhism was based on the teachings of Guru Nanak and grew to include the teachings of the nine subsequent gurus. Guru Nanak laid down that Sikhs were neither Muslim nor Hindu and that they follow the middle path.

Guru Nanak was imprisoned by the Mughal emperor Babar in 1520 for preaching equality of all and monotheism. Guru Arjan Dev, the fifth Sikh guru, was martyred in

1606 by order of the Mughal emperor Jehangir; Chandu, a Hindu, had lodged a report against him for indulging in practices that were alien to both Hinduism and Islam.

Guru Nanak started the practice of langar, community dining regardless of caste or creed. The fourth guru, Guru Ram Das, started the construction of the Darbar Sahib, or Golden Temple. The foundation stone was laid by Mian Mir, a famous Sufi saint, in Guru Arjan Dev's time. Guru Arjan went on to build the Golden Temple. Thus, Amritsar (literally, pool of nectar) was founded and became a gathering point for people from all walks of life and the Sikh sangat, a body of men and women congregating, especially in the presence of the Guru Granth Sahib. In 1604, Guru Arjan compiled the Guru Granth Sahib, which included the teachings of the four previous gurus along with his own, and installed it in the Darbar Sahib, making it the hub of the Sikhs.

The persecution of non-Muslims continued and so the sixth guru, Hargobind, took up arms against the state, doing everything a non-Muslim was not so far permitted, that is, riding horses, carrying swords, and wearing a plume. He set up the Akal Takhth (literally, the throne of the immortal) opposite the Darbar Sahib to emphasize the greatness of God above all. He carried two swords—symbolically called Miri and Piri—to denote temporal and spiritual power that they needed to go hand in hand. The seventh and eighth gurus carried these principles forward, emphasizing on sewa (service) and piety. Guru Teg Bahadur, the ninth guru, taught the Sikhs what the essence of man should be and was the founder of what is akin to the human rights movement today. Like Guru Arjan Dev, he too, laid down his life for the preservation of these rights. The tenth guru, Guru Gobind Singh, gave a form to this religious order founded by Guru Nanak and created the 'Khalsa' (literally, the pure). He incorporated his father Guru Teg Bahadur's baani (teachings) in the Guru Granth Sahib and bestowed the gaddi (seat) of guruship to the Granth Sahib, henceforth to be recognized as the living guru.

Guru Gobind Singh spent his life fighting against persecution and for the rights of the Sikhs, losing his sons and ultimately, his own life in this fight. With the Guru Granth Sahib as the guru now, Banda Singh Bahadur, the Sikh military commander, carried on the battle to protect the Sikhs after Guru Gobind Singh. Born in 1670 he lived the life of an ascetic at Nanded until 1708, when he met Guru Gobind Singh and became his disciple. He assembled a force for the guru leading the struggle against the Mughal Empire. He founded the first Sikh sovereign state with the capital at Lohgarh (literally, fort of steel) and minted the first coins (Nanakshahi sikkas). In 1709, Baba Deep Singh, head of the Sheedan misls and the first head of the Damdami taksal, joined Banda Singh Bahadur during the assaults on the towns of Sadhaura and Sirhind. In 1710, Banda Bahadur captured Sirhind and killed Governor Wazir Khan, who had been responsible for the martyrdom of the two youngest sons of Guru Gobind Singh.

He abolished feudalism and the zamindari system, giving the land back to the peasant and the tiller, which until then had belonged to the state.

Eventually, Banda Bahadur was captured and martyred in the most brutal manner by the Mughals in Delhi. Thereafter, the Sikhs faced the greatest tyranny in their history and, for the first time in the subcontinent, the ingress of foreign invaders was challenged by the Sikhs, at great cost to their lives. In 1757, Ahmed Shah Abdali attacked and destroyed the Harmandir Sahib because the Sikhs had been obstructing his plundering of India. They would harass his troops and rescue countless Hindu women from the marauders' clutches. Baba Deep Singh led the Sikh forces against Abdali's armies and was martyred while fighting to protect the Harmandir Sahib in the Battle of Amritsar at Gohalwar. In 1762, Ahmed Shah Abdali blew up the Darbar Sahib again, and then again in 1764. The Sikhs had got under his skin, for they fought him tirelessly time and again to protect their identity and people. His invasions were too much for the Sikhs to take; they put up such great resistance that they effectively ended invasions from the north. They became virtual masters of the Punjab, the sui generis sovereigns, achieving sovereignty in 1799 when the Sukarchakiya misl under Charat Singh and Maha Singh, respectively the grandfather and father of Maharaja Ranjit Singh, gained predominance over the other misls.[1] My ancestors Surja Singh and Sada Singh were their companions, and rode in triumph into Lahore, alongside Maharaja Ranjit Singh in 1799, when the second sovereign Sikh state and empire was created.

This state was secular and incorporated the Afghan provinces of Peshawar and Kashmir as well as Ladakh, up to Tibet and China. It had diplomatic relations with Great Britain, France, and Russia, the three leading powers of Europe. The Sikh rulers, sensing danger from the British East India Company, engaged European generals who had fought under Napoleon to train their infantry, artillery, and cavalry along European military patterns.

Thus, during the lifetime of Ranjit Singh, the state put an end to any British ambitions of extending their rule beyond the Sutlej river. The only weakness of this modern state was that though it introduced the Western concept of maintaining an army and introduced Western cultural life amongst the Sikhs, Maharaja Ranjit Singh failed

---

[1] The twelve sovereign states in the Sikh Confederacy that rose during the eighteenth century in Punjab.

to introduce the most important concept of European democracy—an elected Parliament—which ultimately proved to be the undoing of this great Sikh empire.

The British annexed the state in 1849, declaring in the treaty signed at the time that when Duleep Singh, son of Maharaja Ranjit Singh, gained majority, the throne would be restored to him. This meant that the sovereignty of the Sikhs was suspended but not abrogated. The British, however, did not keep their word and instead kidnapped the child maharaja, Duleep Singh, sent him to England, converted him to Christianity, and stole the Kohinoor diamond from the darbar's treasury, which Lord Dalhousie then sent to Queen Victoria as a gift from her Indian empire.

In 1947, when the British under their Labour Party government headed by Prime Minister Clement Atlee parted with their Indian empire, there were three contestants to the legacy of the British empire: the Muslim League, the Congress, primarily Hindu, and the Shiromani Akali Dal.

In the nineteenth and twentieth centuries, the Sikhs had struggled for their own identity and a place in the sun, culminating in the British government forming and constituting through a statute the Shiromani Gurdwara Prabandhak Committee (SGPC), elected through universal suffrage of the Sikhs. Founded in 1925, it came to be called the Parliament of Sikhs.

In 1946, the Sikh parliament (SGPC) by a unanimous resolution passed a motion for a separate sovereign independent Sikh state. The British government bypassed all democratic considerations and the historic treaty of 1849 whereby Sikh sovereignty was to be restored, did not honour the SGPC, and divided India between the Hindus and Sikhs, while giving what became Pakistan to the Muslims.

In 1947, a Constituent Assembly was formed to frame the Constitution of India. Two Sikh representatives, Sardar Hukam Singh and Sardar Bhupinder Singh Mann, were taken on board the Constituent Assembly. Going through the debates, the Sikh representatives came to see that the leadership, under Gandhi, Nehru, and Patel would not honour the assurances given to the Sikhs before the dissolution of the British Empire. Article 25 of the present Constitution, in fact, mentions Sikhism as part of the Hindu religion, and the two Sikh representatives thus refused to affix their signatures to the Constitution of India.

The storming of the Golden Temple in 1984 and subsequent genocide of Sikhs following the assassination of Prime Minister Indira Gandhi by her Sikh bodyguards was the proverbial last straw for the Sikhs.

My father keeps a diary. Since we were children, as far back as I can remember, one would see him writing away fastidiously in his little golf diary at the end of the day. In these diaries every little detail is recorded from the interesting to the mundane. This I know, for once in Bombay, I snooped through it, not because I really wanted to pry but because Papa would force Virji and me to keep a diary of our everyday lives. This was quite a task because our lives were pretty ordinary and nothing momentous happened really that one could write about every day. So I would write, '. . . woke up in the morning at such and such time, kissed Mama Papa goodbye, walked to school, or took the bus,' and on and on . . . nothing extraordinary seemed to happen. One day Papa asked to read Virji's and my diaries to check if we really were recording our lives. Not really thinking of it as an invasion of my privacy, I handed mine over to Papa. After reading a few pages, he looked at me with disappointment in his eyes, 'Pitsy, surely you have more to write about than your timetable day after day? Do try and improve your writing and make it a little more interesting.' And so I peeked into his diary, lying on his bedside table when no one was around.

So when I started writing this book, I started asking the family for these little gems that my father was in the habit of filling page upon page. Slowly I came upon a few from Mama's trunks, in musty stores at Pind and a few from Chhote Bhuaji who had carefully preserved his diaries from prison. Most of his diary is on loose sheets of paper, a lot of it lost. Some that I found of his time in prison, are here. What I have managed to recover is from 1987 onwards, by which time he had already been in prison for almost three years. Whether there were earlier ones I don't know, but what I could get my hands on I read through, sometimes with a heavy lump in my throat. Papa's diary helped me understand the man he is and mostly, they helped fill the gaps of the missing years.

The Prison Diaries

Bhagalpur, 31 October 1987

The drama of life and death takes place within the four walls of the prison. They have all provisions to meet any contingency. They can deliver a child, they feed and clothe the inmates, provide medical aid, and in the event of death, they dispose of the body. They also hang people and terminate life. They are both humane and savages. They do all this with characteristic finesse and élan.

I have not found it pleasant here.

A silly clod, one of the juveniles who sweeps the floor in

my cell, took away an empty bottle and was intercepted by Kripa Shankar Panday, the assistant jailor on duty from 6 a.m. to 9 a.m. Panday, in his melodramatic manner, tried to make a mountain out of a molehill, beat the boy, confiscated the bottle, and sent it to the watch tower. Of course, nothing came of it and the chief head warder and the jailor dismissed the matter.

I sat and listened to the cricket commentary between India and New Zealand, feeling disturbed after the morning's events. Ram Shukal was 'sugary sweet and all things nice' when he came on duty from 3 p.m. to 6 p.m. I chose to ignore him.

Yesterday I had complained about him to the jailor for harassing Geeta when she'd come to see me. So I guess from his present manner that he must have been ticked of by the superintendent.

2 November 1987

Kripa Shankar Panday has been transferred to another jail to command it independently. I don't think he'll last for more than a month. He's too gauche. The authorities had the trees pruned drastically and the courtyard outside my cell now looks much bigger than before. I stayed indoors as I could not bear the sight of heavy axes cutting the strong, sturdy branches of the trees I had come to love. It's quite sad.

Later I asked a warder why the branches were being cut. Without answering, he walked away with a mysterious smile, which reminded me of the he-wolf in 'Red Riding Hood': 'All the better to see you with, my dear'.

So now the CRPF men on the tower had an unobstructed view of me all the time.

Khushwant Singh wrote in yesterday's *Hindustan Times* magazine (Sunday) that I was one of the contenders for the post of the chief minister of Punjab. I had a good laugh. Here I was sitting locked up, all alone, heavily guarded night and day, miles and miles away from Punjab, here because of what I believe in, and people were speculating on what I could or could not become.

4 November 1987

The jailor came and said that my wife was here and asked whether I would like to see her. What a silly question, I thought, of course I would, I said. The jailor went but no one came to escort me to meet Geeta. I waited and waited in vain.

In the evening I was sent some goodies that Geeta had brought, the yellow shawl, papads, apples, a torch—a beautiful red one—toothbrushes and toothpaste and several other little things. The lemon drops I'd asked Geeta for weren't there.

5 November 1987

Guru Nanak Sahib's birthday. I said a quiet prayer. The jailor, Satish Babu, came. He said that I'd be appearing in court on the 6th, that is, tomorrow, and that Dr Wadhera was in town to see me, according to his information. Sweet of him to tell me, because they're usually very tightlipped. I asked for candles, which they sent. In the evening, I lit the ward with the candles, the only thing I could do to celebrate Guru Sahib's birthday since I'm not allowed a religious service. The courtyard looked very pretty. Then I was locked in my cell for the night.

6 November 1987

It's court today and the security arrangements just about took the cake. There were very many more vehicles in our cavalcade from the jail to the courts, and CRPF and a BMP [Border Military Police] company were on full alert, stenguns and machine guns and old. 303 rifles, pistols and revolvers in holsters. As the convoy reached the other jail to fetch my fellow so-called accomplices, the DIG joined us too in his car. I noticed there was a new company of CRPF here . . . all to guard me.

I met Bibiji, Dillo Bhenji, and Geeta, none of whom I could embrace. I bowed to the judge before getting into the dock and he graciously acknowledged it. I asked the judge for time to speak to my lawyers, which he allowed. I was writing down the points I wanted my lawyers to pay attention to, when a deputy SP came and said I mustn't write. I asked why. He said I had asked the judge for a meeting and not time for writing. I was pretty amused and told him he was splitting hairs over nothing and in any case, he was in contempt of court for speaking to me directly instead of the prosecutor. Then he approached the judge who dismissed him impatiently and instructed my lawyers to keep taking down my notes . . . waste of precious time.

Geeta very sweetly stood behind me with her hand on my back all this time, probably to restrain me from flaring up. Later, Bibiji gave me a scarf and asked me to tie it around my neck so I did and she handed me some cardamoms, probably blessed by some saint. To please her I kept those too. Then we said our goodbyes. Bibiji and Geeta walked by my side down to the waiting bus and we parted sadly. Kamikar Singh, Charan Singh, Ragbir Singh, and Jagpal Singh were unloaded at the camp jail and I was taken further on to my prison. Then the jailor asked me to deposit with him the scarf and other goodies, as well as the bag of vegetables and of course, I never saw them again. Satish Babu told me later that the police officer accompanying me was asked to certify them but he didn't so they were sent back with him. He also confirmed that the DM had accompanied the IG to my barrack. The DM had told Geeta that he'd met me, but he hadn't. LIES.

10 November 1987

Ram Shukal Singh was on duty from 6 a.m. to 9 p.m. and he was pacing up and down like a man possessed. He looked desperate. I meditated but didn't say my prayers because since yesterday I've had a headache which won't go away.

16 November 1987

My migraine isn't any better despite the Saridon I had last night, which the doctor finally sent me after I had complained for two days. I have sent a request to the jailor to send for a specialist for I don't think a Saridon, Celin and vitamin B which Dr Deo has given me are good enough to take care of the excruciating pain in my head. Ram Shukal, the assistant jailor, has gone away on leave. I have been informed that he's been selling clothes to the prisoners from the clothing godown. That explains why he was looking so agitated a few days ago. I was informed that the lady superintendent's office will be henceforth used to search my wife and other lady relatives before they meet me. That's a change. Thank God.

I had all my clothes washed, bedsheets and all, and they're hanging on the line fluttering in the breeze with the sun beating down upon them. White as snow they look. I asked Ganguli Babu, on duty from twelve noon to three in the afternoon to inform the jailor that my migraine hadn't got any better and to call for Dr Prasad, head of Bhagalpur Medical College. He said he would.

I have been thinking of my wife and children all day today. How I love them all. The pain of not being with them gnaws at me constantly.

19 November 1987

The medical professor from the Bhagalpur Medical College came to check me, a Dr R.N. Sinha, a junior doctor. He took my ECG and said it was normal. He prescribed some medicines for the pain in my right temple and said it would soon be better. Dr S.P. Saha, the dental surgeon, examined my upper jaw, the last but one molar, and wrote it needed grinding. Dr Khan, the jail doctor, didn't want him to write the word 'grinding' as he felt it couldn't be done here. Nevertheless, the dental surgeon stood firm and wrote this.

20 November 1987

The jailor has developed homosexual relations with a

warder, named Maujar Hussain, whom he's been keeping in his house. The DM has got wind of this and he's told the jail superintendent to warn the jailor and his paramour. Maujar Hussain no longer hangs around the jailor's house and now performs his duties in the jail. The jailor is gay, and the mali whom he keeps as his cook is his companion. Interesting little anecdotes I keep hearing about the jail, of hardly any great consequence, but then what else can I be told?

Incidentally, the green pigeons (harials) were sighted by me atop a pipal in my barrack on the 5th of this month. They don't peck at the fruit on the pipal because of the watch tower, where a CRPF jawan is always posted. The Sikh CRPF jawan, the fair-complexioned one who was here last year and who held me in great reverence, is under inquiry because they say he used to salute me. The scope of his inquiry has been extended to his parents and relatives, and his religious and political alignments.

The government is getting far too paranoid, even the CRPF company deployed here now had two Sikhs in it who have been packed off to serve elsewhere. The pain in my right temple has decreased and I can now move my head without too much pain. It's healing without medication. But since the medication has arrived today I shall have it just to be on the safe side. They've sent me a hot-water bottle as well. Small wonders shall never cease.

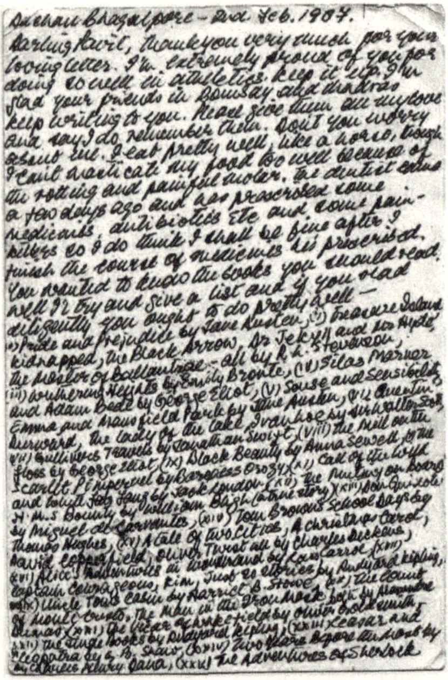

[illegible] Bhagalpore – 2nd Feb. 1987.

Darling Pavit, Thank you very much for your loving letter. I'm extremely proud of you for doing so well in athletics. Keep it up. I'm glad your friends in Bombay and Madras keep writing to you. Please give them all my love and say I do remember them. Don't you worry about me. I eat pretty well, like a horse, though I can't masticate my food too well because of the rotting and painful molar. The dentist came a few days ago and has prescribed some medicines, antibiotics etc and some pain-killers so I do think I shall be fine after I finish the course of medicines he prescribed. You wanted to know the books you should read. Well I'll try and give a list and if you read diligently you ought to do pretty well — (i) Treasure Island, Kidnapped, The Black Arrow, Dr Jekyll and Mr Hyde, The Master of Ballantrae — all by R.L. Stevenson, (ii) Pride and Prejudice by Jane Austen, (iii) Wuthering Heights by Emily Bronte, (iv) Silas Marner and Adam Bede by George Eliot, (v) Sense and Sensibility, Emma and Mansfield Park by Jane Austen, (vi) Quentin Durward, The Lady of the Lake, Ivanhoe by Sir Walter Scott, (vii) Gulliver's Travels by Jonathan Swift, (viii) The Mill on the Floss by George Eliot, (ix) Black Beauty by Anna Sewell, (x) The Scarlet Pimpernel by Baroness Orczy, (xi) Call of the Wild and White Fang by Jack London, (xii) The Mutiny on Board H.M.S. Bounty by William Bligh (a true story), (xiii) Don Quixote by Miguel de Cervantes, (xiv) Tom Brown's School Days by Thomas Hughes, (xv) A Tale of Two Cities, A Christmas Carol, David Copperfield, Oliver Twist all by Charles Dickens, (xvi) Alice's Adventures in Wonderland by Lewis Carrol, (xvii) Just So Stories by Rudyard Kipling, Kim, Captain Courageous, (xix) Uncle Tom's Cabin by Harriet B. Stowe, (xx) The Count of Monte Cristo, The Man in the Iron Mask both by Alexandre Dumas, (xxi) The Vicar of Wakefield by Oliver Goldsmith, (xxii) The Jungle Books by Rudyard Kipling, (xxiii) Caesar and Cleopatra by G.B. Shaw, (xxiv) Two Years Before the Mast by Richard Henry Dana, (xxv) The Adventures of Sherlock

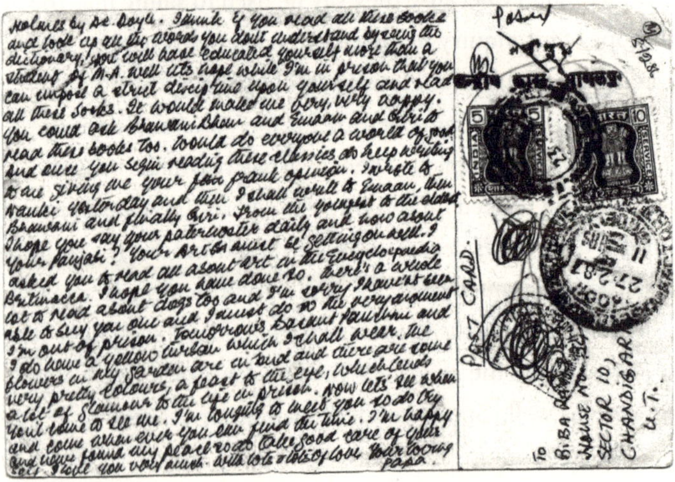

Holmes by Dr. Doyle. I think if you read all these books and look up all the words you don't understand by using the dictionary, you will have educated yourself more than a student of M.A. Well let's hope while I'm in prison that you can impose a strict discipline upon yourself and read all these books. It would make me very, very happy. You could ask Bhawani Bhaw and Emaan and Giri to read these books too. Would do everyone a world of good and once you begin reading these classics, do keep writing to me giving me your own frank opinion. I wrote to Nanki yesterday and then I shall write to Emaan, then Bhawani and finally Giri, from the youngest to the eldest. I hope you say your paternoster daily and how about your Panjabi? Your Art too must be getting on well. I asked you to read all about Art in the Encyclopaedia Britannica. I hope you have done so. There's a whole lot to read about dogs too and I'm sorry I haven't been able to buy you one and I must do so the very moment I'm out of prison. Tomorrow's Basant Panchmi and I do have a yellow turban which I shall wear. The flowers in my garden are in bloom and there are some very pretty colours, a feast to the eye, which lends a lot of glamour to the life in prison. Now let's see when you'll come to see me. I'm longing to meet you so do try and come whenever you can find the time. I'm happy and have found my peace so take good care of yourself. I love you very much. With lots & lots of love. Your loving Papa.

POST CARD.

To Biba [illegible]
House No. [illegible]
Sector 10,
Chandigarh
U.T.

Letter to me

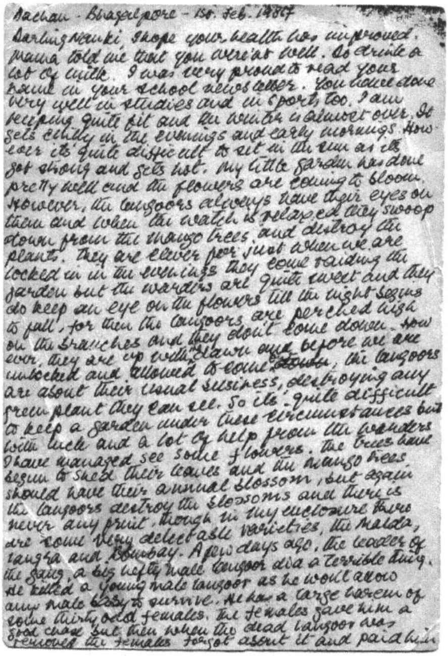

Bachau - Bhagalpore - 15th Feb. 1987
Darling Nanki, I hope your health has improved.
Mama told me that you weren't well. Do drink a
lot of milk. I was very proud to read your
name in your school newsletter. You have done
very well in studies and in sports, too. I am
keeping quite fit and the winter is almost over. It
gets chilly in the evenings and early mornings. How-
ever it's quite difficult to sit in the sun as its
got strong and gets hot. My little garden has done
pretty well and the flowers are coming to bloom.
However, the langoors always have their eyes on
them and when the watch is relaxed they swoop
down from the mango trees and destroy the
plants. They are clever for just when we are
locked in in the evenings they come raiding the
garden but the warders are quite sweet and they
do keep an eye on the flowers till the night begins
to fall, for then the langoors are perched high
on the branches and they don't come down. How
ever, they are up with dawn and before we are
unlocked and allowed to come down, the langoors
are about their usual business, destroying any
green plant they can see. So its quite difficult
to keep a garden under these circumstances but
with luck and a lot of help from the warders
I have managed see some flowers. The trees have
begun to shed their leaves and the mango trees
should have their annual blossom, but again
the langoors destroy the blossoms and there is
never any fruit, though in my enclosure there
are some very delectable varieties, the Malda,
Langra and Bombay. A few days ago, the leader of
the gang, a big hefty male langoor did a terrible thing.
He killed a young male langoor as he won't allow
any male baby to survive. He has a large harem of
some thirty odd females. The females gave him a
good chase but then when the dead langoor was
removed the females forgot about it and paid him

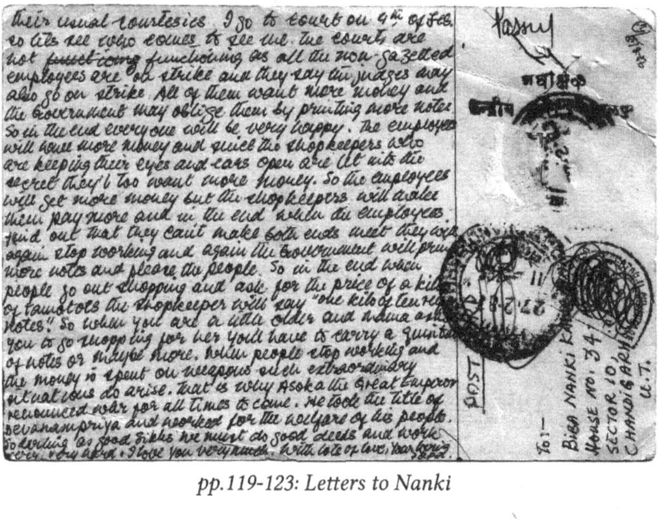

their usual courtesies. I go to court on 4th of Feb.
so lets see who comes to see me. The courts are
not ~~functioning~~ functioning as all the non-gazetted
employees are on strike and they say the judges may
also go on strike. All of them want more money and
the Government may oblige them by printing more notes.
So in the end everyone will be very happy. The employees
will have more money and since the shopkeepers also
are keeping their eyes and ears open are let into the
secret they'l too want more money. So the employees
will get more money but the shopkeepers will make
them pay more and in the end when the employees
find out that they can't make both ends meet they will
again stop working and again the Government will print
more notes and please the people. So in the end when
people go out shopping and ask for the price of a kilo
of tomatoes the shopkeeper will say "one kilo of ten re[ams of]
notes." So when you are a little older and mama asks
you to go shopping for her you'll have to carry a quintal
of notes or maybe more. When people stop working and
the money is spent on weapons such extraordinary
situations do arise. That is why Asoka the Great Emperor
renounced war for all times to come. He took the title of
Devanampriya and worked for the welfare of his people.
So darling as good Sikhs we must do good deeds and work
very very hard. I love you very much. With lots of love, Your loving
Papa.

To:-
Biba Nanki K[...]
House No. 34,
Sector 10,
Chandigarh
U.T.

pp.119-123: Letters to Nanki

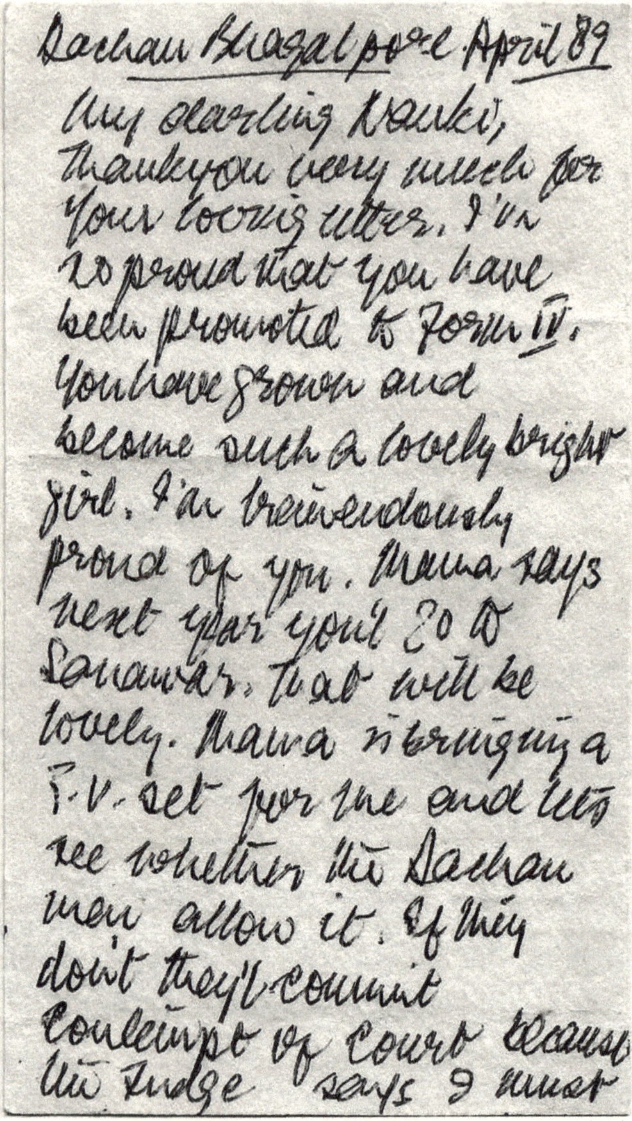

Dachau Bhagalpore April 89

My darling Nanki,

Thankyou very much for your loving letter. I'm so proud that you have been promoted to Form IV. You have grown and become such a lovely bright girl. I'm tremendously proud of you. Mama says next year you'll go to Sanawar. That will be lovely. Mama is bringing a T.V. set for me and let's see whether the Dachau men allow it. If they don't they'll commit contempt of court because the Judge says I must

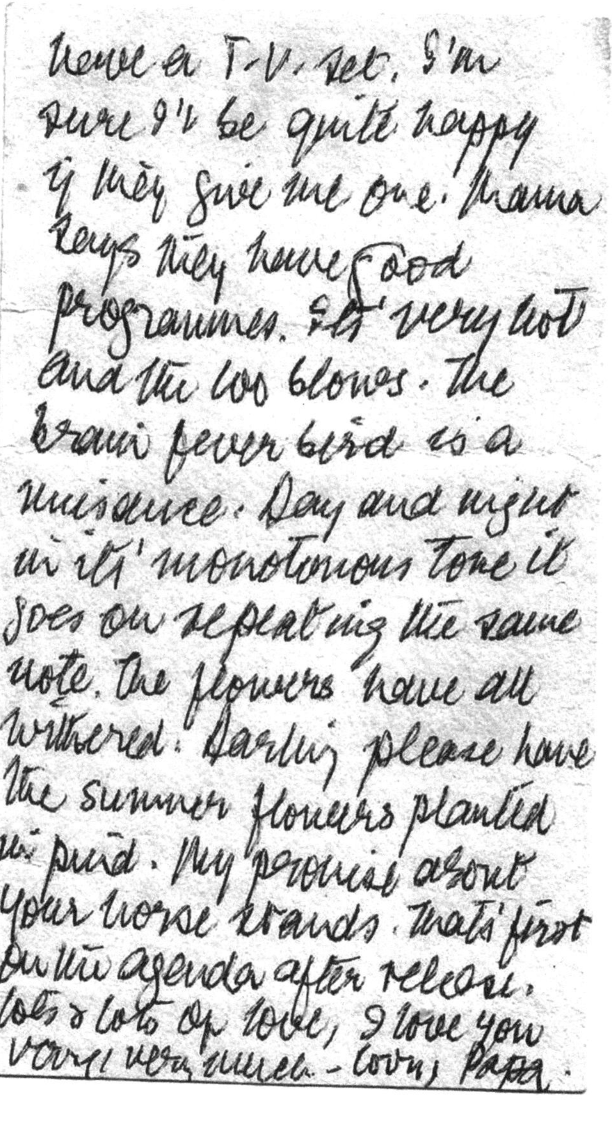

have a T.V. set. I'm sure I'll be quite happy if they give me one. Mama says they have good programmes. It's very hot and the loo blows. The brain fever bird is a nuisance. Day and night in its monotonous tone it goes on repeating the same note. The flowers have all withered. Darling please have the summer flowers planted in Pindi. My promise about your horse stands. That's first on the agenda after release. Lots & lots of love, I love you very very much. – Love, Papa.

Darling Nanki, I didn't write to you last time as the mail was
about to leave and I had to seal the envelope quickly
so that it would leave the Darbar in good, safe hands.
Did you read about Mr. Shikapa? This time round I
write to you about my friend Sriram who was from
Trinidad, West Indies. It's an island about 10° north of the
equator, north of Venezuela in the Caribbean Sea, which is in the
Atlantic Ocean. Longitude wise it lies 60°W so when you look
it up in the atlas you'll know exactly where it is for it's a
tiny little island, rich with sugarcane plantations. Now of course
oil and asphalt have replaced sugar as its main product and
item of export. It's in the Commonwealth and the people there
play cricket very well. In the 19th century the British took a
lot of labourers from here in Behar to work the sugar
plantations and Sri Sriram's great, great grand parents had
obviously gone there from here. As time passed his forefathers
ceased to be labourers and through hard work came to own
their own plantation so when Sriram was a child ~~they~~ his
~~wanted~~ parents wanted to send their son to their ~~home~~ native
country and study there. Here in India he was sent to
Bishop Cotton School and he was put in the same house, Lefroy
as me. We became friends. He was very shy and would hardly
talk because being a foreigner and somewhat blacker than
the others he found himself at odds with India and his old
ancestoral country. He had gleaming white teeth, a very dark
skin of deep brown, wiry, thick hair and since we thought ~~it~~ he
had an odd name Sreeram we decided to call him Trini,
Trini for short for Trinidad. As ~~he~~ we became friends ~~and~~ he
began to get chirpy. One day he showed me his family album and
his house on their family plantation. He had two little sisters,
darker than him, a baby brother who was in his mothers arms and
who also joined B.C.S. the year we passed out and there was Trini
held his father by his hand. It was a lovely family photograph
but what surprised and horrified me was that Trini's father had
one leg missing. From beneath his shorts I could see just one
leg. And I said to Trini why his dad had just one leg. So this is
what Trini said. He told me that his father was the best
~~cricketer~~ cricketer and swimmer in his school. In ~~to~~ Trinidad
~~they~~ they play cricket on the beach and when the tide ebbs they
find it ideal to lay the wickets and begin batting and
bowling. When his father was batting, the bowler bowled a
nice juicy ball on his leg wicket and his father reached out

out to it, caught it to full toss and took a full blooded
sweep with his bat and sent it hurtling into the sea.
Amongst them its a rule that if you send the ball into the sea,
its not fielder who fetches it but the batsman for the sea
is infested with sharks. The other rule is that if you don't
want to fetch the ball you pay for the ball and the game starts
thitherto. Trini's father, because being the best cricketer and a
swimmer opted to go out into the sea and retrieve the
ball. He took off the few clothes he was wearing because in the
tropics they wear very few clothes and plunged into the sea. He
swam out, riding the current as the sea was ebbing. But
since it was ebbing the ball also went farther and farther
away. Trini's dad using all his skill and strength of the best
swimmer finally got to the ball but by then it was too late as
he was too far out into the sea and he could see a pair of
fins racing towards him. He knew from experience that
that was a shark and so he dropped the ball and made
all speed for the beach. His powerful arms and his skills
were of little use as he was swimming against the current
for the sea was ebbing. But he didn't give up hope and
drawing upon every ounce of energy he struck out at the
water making for home. But the shark was swiftly closing the
gap but Trini's dad didn't lose hope and in the teeth of
adversity paddled even harder and this resolve was
probably what saved his life. His friends came out to
distract the shark but the creature was single minded and
after this very quarry. But his dad paddled on, the shark now
just a few feet away and looking as hungry and evil as
only sharks do. As he was about to hit the shallows the shark
struck with deadly accuracy and single minded determination
and sliced off his dads leg from the thigh downwards. His
friends rushed him to hospital in a pool of blood but since
the hospital was quite used to such casualties the doctor
on emergency duty knew exactly what to do. He cleaned the wound,
bandaged it and gave Trini's dad powerful shots of
antibiotics. His leg was gone forever, eaten by a shark and he
was never to play cricket again but he never gave up
swimming. His dad came to India once, when Trini's younger
brother joined school and besides Trini I was the only one to
know how his dad had lost a leg. Your Amiji knows Trini but
as Sriram for he would come and spend his winter holidays
with me at Pune. Next time another story (true). I love you very
very much. Lots & lots of love. Your loving Papa.

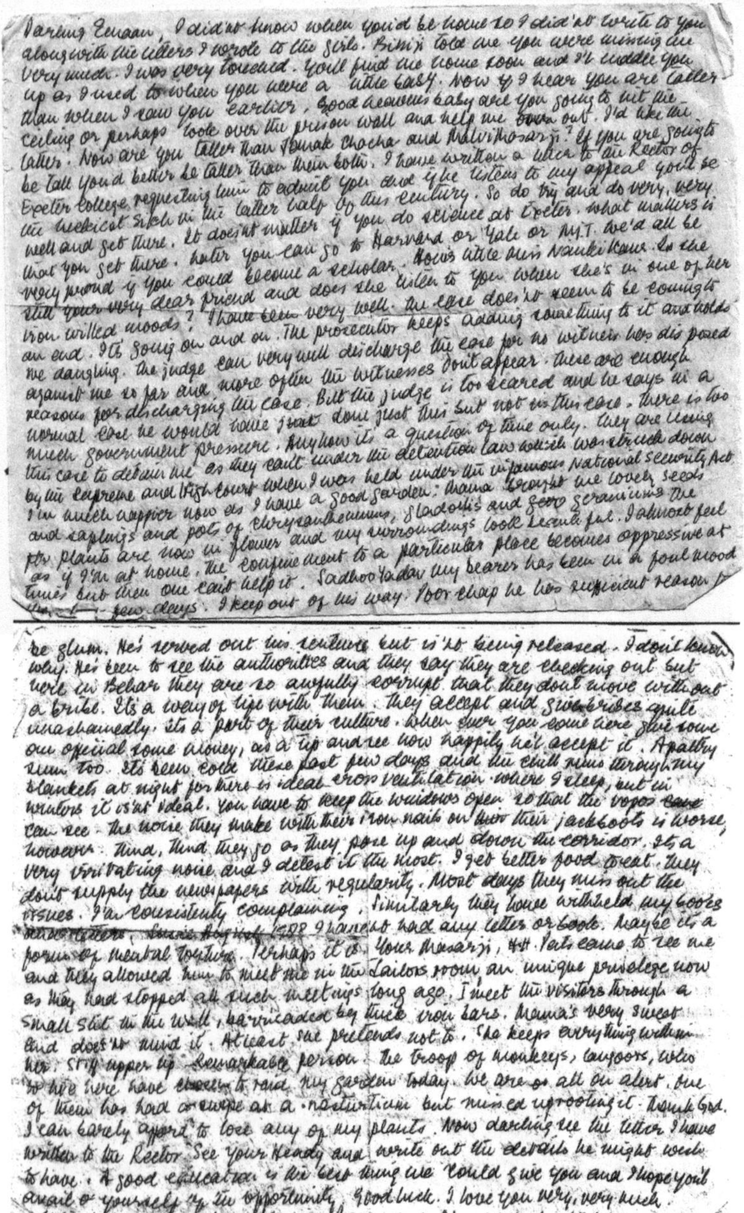
Darling Emaan, I didn't know when you'd be home so I didn't write to you
alongwith the letters I wrote to the girls. Bimiji told me you were missing me
very much. I was very touched. You'll find me home soon and I'll cuddle you
up as I used to when you were a little baby. Now if I hear you are taller
than when I saw you earlier, Good heavens baby are you going to hit the
ceiling or perhaps look over the prison wall and help me bown out. I'd like the
latter. Now are you taller than Tomak Chacha and Malvimosarji? If you are going to
be tall you'd better be taller than them both. I have written a letter to the Rector of
Exeter College requesting him to admit you and if he listens to my appeal you'll be
the medical Sikh in the latter half of this century. So do try and do very, very
well and get there. It doesn't matter if you do science at Exeter. What matters is
that you get there. Later you can go to Harvard or Yale or M.I.T. We'd all be
very proud if you could become a scholar. How's little Miss Nanki Kaur. Is she
still your very dear friend and does she listen to you when she's in one of her
iron willed moods? I have been very well. The case doesn't seem to be coming to
an end. It's going on and on. The prosecutor keeps adding something to it and holds
me dangling. The judge can very well discharge the case for no witness has disposed
against me so far and more often the witnesses don't appear. There are enough
reasons for discharging the case. But the judge is too scared and he says in a
normal case he would have just done just this but not in this case. There is too
much government pressure. Anyhow it's a question of time only. They are using
this case to detain me as they can't under the detention law which was struck down
by the supreme and High Court when I was held under the infamous National Security Act.
I'm much happier now as I have a good garden. Mama brought me lovely seeds
and saplings and pots of chrysanthemums, gladiolis and geraniums. The
few plants are now in flower and my surroundings look beautiful. I almost feel
as if I'm at home. The confinement to a particular place becomes oppressive at
times but then one can't help it. Sadhoo Yadav my bearer has been in a foul mood
the last few days. I keep out of his way. Poor chap he has sufficient reason to
be glum. He's served out his sentence but is'nt being released. I don't know
why. He's been to see the authorities and they say they are checking out but
here in Behar they are so awfully corrupt that they don't move without
a bribe. It's a way of life with them. They accept and give bribes quite
unashamedly. It's a part of their culture. Whenever you come here give some
official some money, as a tip and see how happily he'll accept it. A paltry
sum too. It's been cold these past few days and the chill runs through my
blankets at night for there is ideal cross ventilation where I sleep, but in
winters it is'nt ideal. You have to keep the windows open so that the cops can
see. The noise they make with their iron nails on their jackboots is worse,
however. Thud, thud they go as they pace up and down the corridor. It's a
very irritating noise and I detest it the most. I get better food to eat. They
don't supply the newspapers with regularity. Most days they miss out the
issues. I'm consistently complaining. Similarly they have withheld my books
~~and letters. Since August 1988~~ I have'nt had any letter or book. Maybe it's a
form of mental torture. Perhaps it is. Your Masarji, H.H. Pat came to see me
and they allowed him to meet me in the Jailors room, an unique privelege now
as they had stopped all such meetings long ago. I meet the visitors through a
small slit in the wall, barricaded by thick iron bars. Mama's very sweet
and does'nt mind it. Atleast she pretends not to. She keeps everything within
her. Stiff upper lip. Remarkable person. The troop of monkeys, langoors, who
live here have chosen to raid my garden today. We are all on alert. One
of them has had a swipe at a nasturtium but missed uprooting it. Thank God.
I can barely afford to lose any of my plants. Now darling see the letter I have
written to the Rector. See your Heady and write out the details he might wish
to have. A good education is the best thing we could give you and I hope you'll
avail yourself of the opportunity. Good luck. I love you very, very much.
Lots & lots of love. Your loving Papa — I have'nt checked the letter.

A letter to Virji

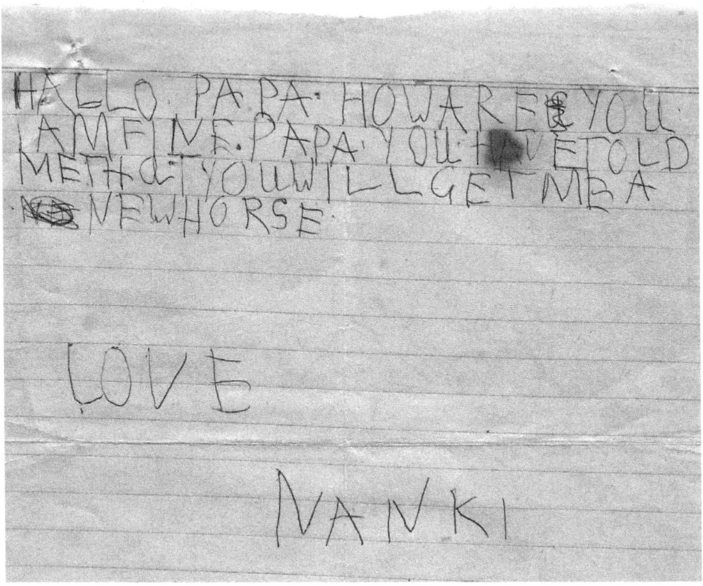

HALLO PAPA HOW ARE YOU
I AM FINE. PAPA YOU HAVE TOLD
ME THAT YOU WILL GET ME A
NEW HORSE

LOVE

NANKI

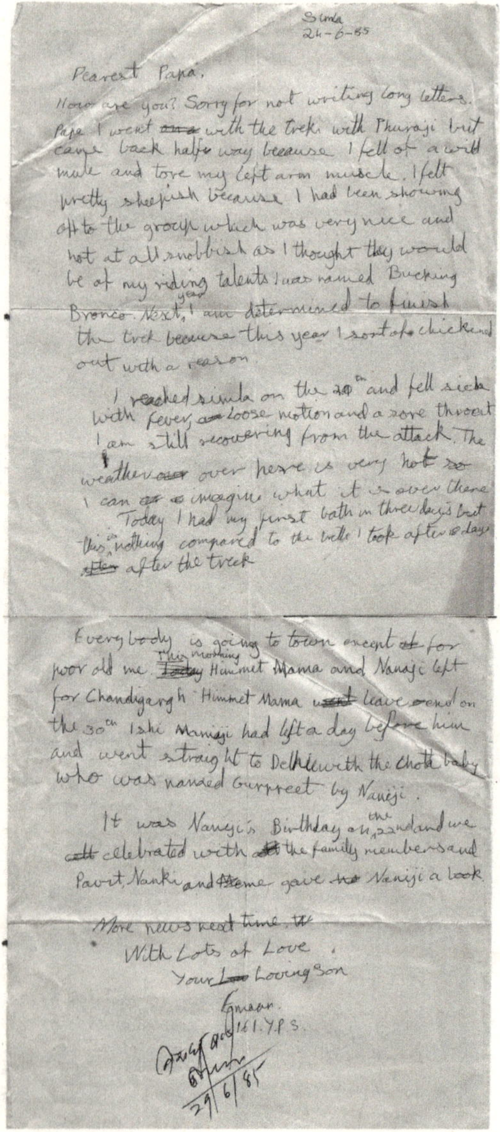

Simla
24-6-85

Dearest Papa,
How are you? Sorry for not writing long letters. Papa I went with the trek with Bhuraji but came back half way because I fell of a wild mule and tore my left arm muscle. I felt pretty sheepish because I had been showing off to the group which was very nice and not at all snobbish as I thought they would be of my riding talents I was named Bucking Bronco. Next year, I am determined to finish the trek because this year I sort of chickened out with a reason.

I reached Simla on the 20th and fell sick with fever, loose motion and a sore throat I am still recovering from the attack. The weather over here is very hot I can imagine what it is over there.

Today I had my first bath in three days but this is nothing compared to the bath I took after 18 days after the trek.

Everybody is going to town except for poor old me. This morning Himmet Mama and Nanaji left for Chandigargh Himmet Mama leave on the 30th Ishi Mamiaji had left a day before him and went straight to Delhi with the chota baby who was named Gurpreet by Naniji.

It was Naniji's Birthday on the 22nd and we celebrated with the family members and Pavit, Nanki and me gave Naniji a book.

More news next time.
With Lots of Love.
Your Loving Son
Gmaar.
161. Y.P.S.

[illegible]
29/6/85

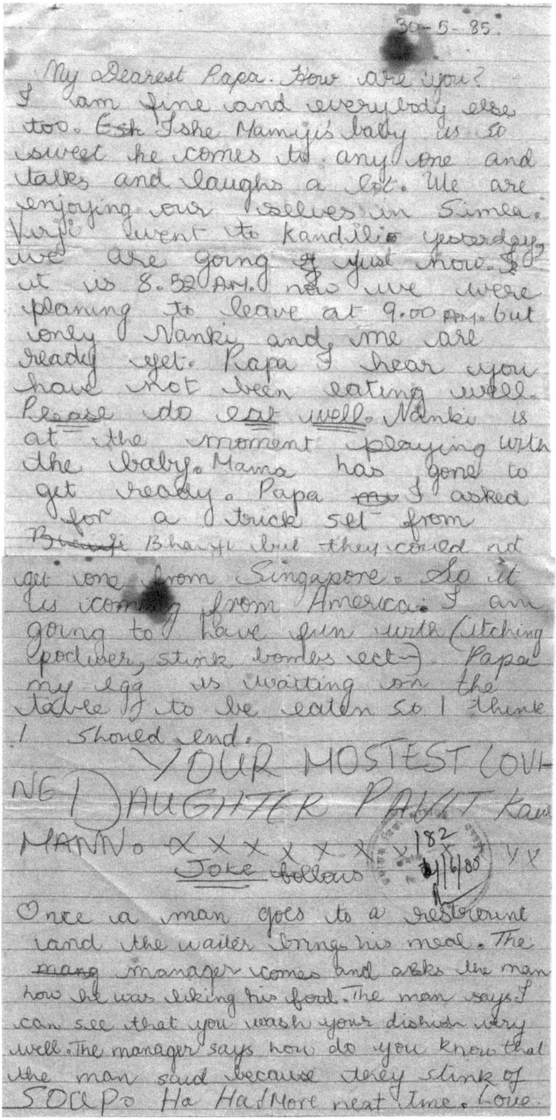

30-5-85.

My Dearest Papa. How are you? I am fine and everybody else too. ~~Esh~~ Ishe Mamiji's baby is so sweet he comes to any one and talks and laughs a lot. We are enjoying our selves in Simla. Virji went to Kandili yesterday, we are going just now. So it is 8.52 A.M. now we were planing to leave at 9.00 A.M. but only Nanki and me are ready yet. Papa I hear you have not been eating well. Please do eat well. Nanki is at the moment playing with the baby. Mama has gone to get ready. Papa ~~m~~ I asked for a trick set from ~~B~~ Bhaiji but they could not get one from Singapore. So it is coming from America. I am going to have fun with (itching powder, stink bombs ect-). Papa my egg is waiting on the table to be eaten so I think I should end.

YOUR MOSTEST LOVING DAUGHTER PAVIT Kaur MANN. x x x x x x x x x

Joke ~~follows~~

182
1/6/85

Once a man goes to a restorunt and the waiter brings his meal. The ~~mang~~ manager comes and asks the man how he was liking his food. The man says I can see that you wash your dishes very well. The manager says how do you know that the man said because they stink of SOAP. Ha Ha! More next time. Love

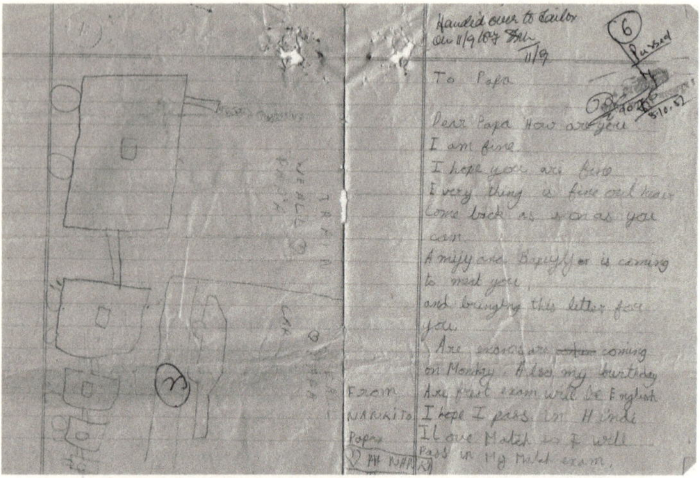

Handed over to Tailor on 11/9/87

11/9

Passed

8.10.87

To Papa

Dear Papa How are you

I am fine.

I hope you are fine

Every thing is fine and [illegible]

Come back as soon as you can.

A mijy and Bapuji [illegible] is coming to meet you,

and bringing this letter for you.

Are exams are coming on Monday. Also my birthday

Are first exam will be English

I hope I pass in Hindi

I love Math so I will pass in My Math exam.

From NANKITO Papa

PH NANKI

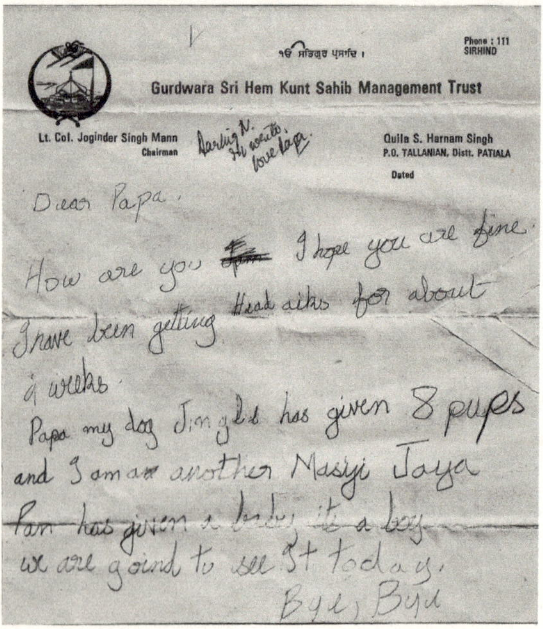

ੴ ਸਤਿਗੁਰ ਪ੍ਰਸਾਦਿ ।

Phone : 111 SIRHIND

Gurdwara Sri Hem Kunt Sahib Management Trust

Lt. Col. Joginder Singh Mann Chairman

Quila S. Harnam Singh P.O. TALLANIAN, Distt. PATIALA

Dated

Darling N. Hi sweets, love Papa.

Dear Papa.

How are you I hope you are fine.

I have been getting Head aiks for about 2 weeks.

Papa my dog Jingle has given 8 pups

and I am another Masiji Jaya ~~Pan has given a baby its a boy~~

we are goind to see It today.

Bye, Bye

25 November 1987

This morning, the assistant jailor on duty from 6 a.m. to 9 a.m. spotted an undertrial prisoner atop the pipal tree opposite my barrack across the road and towards the north. He raced out and caught the poor chap. And I later learnt that he'd been sent to a cell. He must have been beaten badly before being sent into a cell. The assistant jailor told me that he'd asked the man why he'd climbed the tree and he'd said he'd wanted 'to see Mann Singh'. Poor man, his curiosity proved to be disastrous. I feel bad that he got into so much trouble just to catch a glimpse of me. I couldn't concentrate on my prayers the whole day.

26 November 1987

Satish Babu, in charge of the godown, the stuffed-up cock, was here on duty from 6 a.m. to 9 a.m. and he told the warders not to speak with me as it was dangerous and may land them in jail. The warders are sweet and fill me in on all the jail gossip and goings-on. They have scant regard for the jailors or their orders to not talk to me at all. Sweetie-pies.

Bhukal pandit, my pania,[2] left for Pokhar jail where he faces another trial, in another case. He's been replaced

[2] Cook or factotum, all rolled into one.

by another pania—a person called Mandal. Cross-eyed young man.

27 November1987

The jailor and Dr Deo came and the former asked me to get ready for court. They handcuffed me and escorted me to the bus, surrounded and packed with armed CRPF and BMP men. We collected my companions from the camp jail en route. Happy to see them all. We were driven on to the courts. Bibiji, Dads and Teddy Bhayaji were there. Loved meeting them, they said all was well at home.

Bibiji told me that Nanki had done very well in her school athletic meet, winning several medals. I felt very proud of my little baby. She also said that my popularity was at its peak and it would not be long before they released me. Bibiji's been such a great source of strength for me. What a great mother. So strong and steadfast. Dr Wadhera and Binou babu put up a stout defence, defending the venue of the trial, that is, the court and not the jail. The judge allowed me some time with Dr Wadhera, who told me our case would come up in the Supreme Court on 14 December.

November 1987

Benazir Bhutto got married today, aged thirty-four. Met

her at Chandigarh airport in 1972, when she accompanied her father for the Simla talks. She was thin and tall, horsy-looking, the splitting image of her father. She wore a salwar-kameez but no dupatta. Her father Zulfikar Ali Bhutto looked uncomfortable and kept fidgeting. I think he wore a double-breasted cream-coloured suit. Then there was his military secretary. Very fair, with a bulging tummy. He had his pips upside down. I quietly took him aside and pointed this out to him, asking him to wear them correctly. The reception at Chandigarh was utterly shabby and no executive president to my mind has ever been received with such calculated aloofness.

January 1988

Court. Geeta, my joy, Dilloo Bhenji, my anchor, and Teddy Bhayaji, who's never down, were here. Binay babu tore the prosecutor's witness to shreds in his cross-examination. Dilloo Bhenji and Geeta told me that the meeting at Fatehgarh Sahib had been a great success and that the sangat had shouted for my release. Jethmalani told the Akali leaders that they must just put one demand and that should be my release.

5 January 1988

Binay Babu again tore the government's arguments to

shreds. So the evidence ended before lunch. I didn't get much time with my family as I was hurried back to jail.

6 January 1988

Court. The prosecution could not produce their second witness, prosecutor Prasad cut a very sorry figure. The Judge gave me fifteen minutes to speak with my family.

26 February 1988

Haven't been feeling well lately. Bibiji and Dilloo Bhenji came to the gate and I met them for a minute from behind iron bars and wire meshing. I said I'd be coming to court. Satisfied by that, they left. I went to court—my companions told me there was merry hell because I wasn't produced.

29 and 30 March 1988.

I didn't receive a copy of the *Indian Express,* 29 March, and I became suspicious because Ganguli, the assistant jailor, came and told me at 9 p.m. that it hadn't arrived. He looked nervous and I could tell he was telling a lie. Someone on 30 March came and told me that this very newspaper carried the headline that I would be released before Baisakhi. In the evening all the newspapers came, except the previous day's *Indian Express*, and so I told Ram Shukla to go to the jailor and tell him that if I didn't get yesterday's paper I would go on a fast. Then when Gangooli came at 9 p.m. he brought it along and lo and behold, it carried the same article which I'd been informed about. The newspaper was wrinkled and Ganguli had scratched off the date of receipt. I told him directly that the newspaper had arrived yesterday and that he hadn't given it. He denied it but I told him he was telling a lie.

And so life carried on for Papa through 1988 as well. He seems to have kept himself busy with his routine. Books, newspapers, and his little radio were pretty much all he had in the form of entertainment.

In a letter to Chhote Buaji later that year, he writes:

I feel like Yehudi Menuhin conducting the New York Philharmonic and getting the applause he receives at the end of each performance when you come and meet me through that little hole with iron bars. Your visits elate me. Sometimes I do get into the dumps, but if it wasn't for the bashings, how would one appreciate the goodies?

I retire early these days, as the insects are once again a nuisance and they get into my clothes, even my beard.

The greedy geckos that hang around the light bulb are having a field day stuffing themselves sick with insects of every size. One day one of them wanted to grab a bat, frequent visitors. The audacity! I don't mind them having a feast but the after effects are equally sickening. They eat so much and naturally defecate liberally—big droppings all over my table and room. Before I'm locked in for the night, my pania lowers the mosquito flaps and tucks them under the mattress or else the insects get into my bed and then it's impossible to sleep. I mostly just drink a glass of milk and eat a few almonds for supper and then slip into bed and lie and listen to music. Mostly Western classical, till it lulls me to sleep. Last night I was just about to doze off when I heard the Ninth Symphony of Beethoven and I woke up with a start. It's very very loud and bold. Beethoven was stone deaf when he wrote it in 1824 and his last great piece of music. Great musicians like him receive vibrations which they then writeout. Guru Nanak Sahib used to tell Mardana, 'Mardania thuro bani aahie' (teachings from the fountainhead or God).

Schumann, another famous musician, poor man, couldn't understand these strong vibrations and once, in ecstasy, jumped into a river and people thought he was quite mad.

I understand them much more now since I have been in jail and though I took a short course in Western classical music with Geeta, I now appreciate and understand the motivation behind these great masters' works now. So one up for being in the Dachau![3]

In April 1989, the government filed a charge sheet against Papa and three others as co-conspirators: Attinderpal Singh, an activist of the All-India Sikh Students' Federation, and two other Bombay-based college teachers, Jagmohan Singh, alias Toni, thirty years old, professor at Jai Hind College, and Dalip Singh, vice-principal of Khalsa College. Drafted by the Special Investigation Team (SIT), it accused the four of 'criminal conspiracy to wage war against the government and conspiracy to murder Smt. Indira Gandhi'.

Ram Jethmalani, in complete disbelief, said, 'the charge sheet can never stand before any fair judge in a fair trial. Nobody will believe anything the government does now. Nobody should.' He added, 'The SIT has come to stand for the "Sikh Inquisitory Team".'

Bhagalpur 1989

In 1985, the Supreme Court gave me certain facilities like

[3] This is what my father called jail, after the concentration camp in Germany.

a radio, books, visitors, and medical treatment. They've all been denied to me here in Bhagalpur throughout 1986 and only in 1987 was the radio given.

All prisoners here have a religious service once a week. A maulvi comes each Friday for the Muslims and a Brahmin every Sunday for the Hindus and a Christian priest whenever he's called for. For years I have been asking for a religious service, and though the sessions trial court has ordered a service no action is ever taken. Similarly with a TV—the sessions court has passed orders to give me one but the government does not allow either a private one or provide one itself. In the matter of books, too, they have found, amongst various others, the biography of Guru Gobind Singh by Bhai Vir Singh objectionable, and have withheld it.

My visitors are ill-treated and not allowed to meet me with dignity. My aged parents, my wife, and sisters see me through a small slit in the wall with iron bars. My children have been denied access to me and for the last five years I've hardly met them. Emaan and Pavit were turned away from the gate of the jail and poor Emaan was ticked off pretty badly. There is no justice for a Sikh prisoner of conscience (people who have been detained because of their political, religious, or other conscientiously held beliefs. Amnesty International is a great champion of prisoners of conscience.) Now how will I get a fair trial shut up in Tihar Jail?

From the top to the bottom, there is anti-Sikhism and one is as good as lost to the hangman before the beginning of the trial. The electronic media has been whipped up and is going hammer and tongs spreading disinformation about me and taking away the attention from Dhawan, named by Commissioner Thakkar, and several others, whose names are not being revealed. Give the dog a bad name and hang him. Jethmalani is under personal verbal attack, under what mental conditions and frame of mind will he be able to defend me? Will this be a trial? I'll be lynched!

Now I'm posed with the moral dilemma—to stand trial, which is going to be orchestrated, and to fake or reject it and let the bigots proceed ex-parte? We'll have to see.

Poor Geeta is ill now with a slipped disc and can't move. How is the poor lady going to cope with this? What's she done to deserve this? Do writings ever constitute criminal charges for murder? For sedition? For war? Is this a free country? And why can't one express one's feelings when one's holiest shrine has been literally razed to the ground by tanks, artillery, and helicopter air power? Is it a crime to protest? Yes it is. Here I am, facing the music. Let them persecute and kill me. But my words will haunt them forever like Lady Macbeth.

Imagine four and a half years in prison in solitary confinement and now this, another case. This one a murder charge of a prime minister. Can anyone last out such mental pain? I am being driven to the last reservoir of mental and physical strength. Will I make it is the question now. It's the last lap. The last round. If Guru Sahib blesses me with courage and strength, I'll punch my way out or else go down like a good captain of a ship.

I find it warm now, hotter than usual, and feel uncomfortable. I get physically exhausted. It's very very tough now. Last rounds invariably are. My appetite has diminished and I can hardly eat a complete wholesome meal. Fear, uncertainty, and doubts prevail. Can I make it? I'm trying desperately hard for my people and my family, both of whom I love and respect.

10 April 1989

I was pottering around, walking from room to room, for I have five rooms in my barrack and I'm the lone occupant, when Sharma, the clerk on duty, came and told me that I had visitors and I must get ready. So I quickly bathed, brushed my beard, put on a fresh kurta-pyjama, rinsed my mouth with Listerine and sat down to wait. A while later Shukal Babu arrived, with his stomach preceding him, and said that Dr Wadhera (lawyer) and Dilloo Bhenji had come. I was thrilled. Though I was expecting someone to come and see me today, I had forgotten about it.

So I accompanied him to the gate and sat myself down in the jailor's room. Dr Wadhera in a white kurta-pyjama was soon brought in. We had a long talk–he said that the case was a repetition of what had already taken place here. It was registered at the last moment to salvage the government after the Thakkar Commission report was leaked. According to his information, Ritu Sarin, who is close to the Special Investigation Team (SIT) and is writing a book, had said that the majority of SIT officers were against involving me as there was no evidence. S. Charanjit Singh Walia had met Boota Singh, who had said that there was no evidence against me and that this was done because of political pressure.

I told Mr Wadhera to collect the best team of lawyers under Mr Jethmalani. He said Governor Ray had been inquiring how our relations with Mr Jethmalani were because he was considered the biggest enemy of Rajiv Gandhi. I said that that was a gentle hint from Governor Ray to lay off Mr Jethmalani and thus take us away from the best lawyer. In lieu, what had the government done?—its worst and registered this false case. I said I was not prepared to give up Mr Jethmalani. It would show very poor character and then we'd be neither here nor there. Then he said that another strategy was that I fight the case myself and that the government provide me with a library. I said I didn't see how in my present mental condition in prison and solitary confinement I could possibly concentrate on studies.

It was a nice hour-long meeting with Dr Wadhera

and he said he'd come again on April 1989. Then I was allowed to meet Dillo Bhenji through the iron bars. She wore a white dupatta and a dark blue suit and was looking pretty downcast, though she cheered me up immediately by telling me that she'd just received word from Teddy Bhayaji that the bandh called by Baba Joginder Singh to protest the registration of this fresh case against me was a total success. She said that Governor Ray didn't want to give total amnesty and that he wanted to keep Jathedar Tohra behind bars. Gurcharan Singh Tohra was head of the SGPC and an influential and controversial Sikh leader.

I said it would be ridiculous and that I'd not be party to such bargaining. Amnesty meant 'total' and not 'partial'. She said that the Centre was trying for an AISSF[4] government on the pattern of Assam by sidelining the Akalis. They had told the AISSF that I had also been put out of the way, so they may buy the AISSF off. She then told me that M.I. Alam, the SSP of Jullundur, had written to the government that they would need more police officers in Punjab if I was implicated as the situation would become impossible. In spite of this advice, the government has registered this case. She said that H.H. Pats[5] had invited Teddy Bhayaji and herself for lunch and said that he would see that I was made president of the United Akali Dal and that Badal be accepted for the chief

[4] All-India Sikh Students Federation.

[5] His Highness Patiala.

ministership. He said the working committee should have seventeen members each from the three groups (Papa, Talwandi, and Barnala); seventeen from ours, seventeen from Barnala's and seventeen from Talwandi's, making it a fifty-one-member committee. That Badal would be the chairman of the parliamentary board, which would have four members. The members would be recommended by Badal and that I would approve. If I didn't, then he'd suggest another panel. I said I agreed to the formula but that as president I must have more say in the constitution of the parliamentary board.

She said she'd talk further. They would organize more strikes and stop vehicular and rail traffic. She said hundreds of panchayats had already begun sending their representations to the government to withdraw this false case. She said that the Cabinet Committee on Punjab, which visits Chandigarh on April 1989, would be boycotted by all groups and no Akali leader would appear before it as a mark of protest against this case (conspiracy to murder Mrs Indira Gandhi). She told me that I was not to worry and to remain steadfast as this was expected and that now it was done and over with.

All Sikhs had once again united and were on one platform under my leadership. Dillo Bhenji's a sweetie pie and has boosted my morale no end—I felt as robust and strong as a man who lives free in his own country. She said that members of Asia Watch had come to see Sardar

Gurtej Singh and that they'd also met Geeta, who's in bed with a bad disc. She also said that H.H. Pats was going to Germany for a Sikh conference and would do all he could there. And then it was time for us to be parted; she had brought me some tuck, which I collected, touched her feet and gave her a great big hug and then quickly marched back to my barrack escorted by Shukal Babu.

It was a lovely meeting. She's so brave and intelligent. Oh, yes, I told her that Dads must go see Jathedar Tohra, so let's see what comes of that and what they do on Baisakhi. The *Times of India* reported that 'hartals' were total in Tarn Taran, Majitha, Patiala, Bhatinda, Faridkot, and Ferozepur and partial elsewhere. So I must keep my spirits up for all that I have done is for the Panth and the Panth is squarely behind me at this critical juncture.

Dalhousie, 24 August 2010

I am here once again to write. Papa, Mama, I, and the dogs—Rustam, Bhuri, Ameera, and little Abu.

Today is rakhri and Papa has decided to spend the day sleeping. He's tired and is here to recoup after a surgery. The day before he'd gone pelting down the mountain to Chandigarh to be with Chhote Bhuaji because she'd had a stroke.

My Chhote Bhua has been battling cancer this last year. She was Papa's pillar, anchor, and mentor through his time underground and in prison. When I went through all the letters he had written to her from prison—which she has lovingly and carefully preserved—I was a bit surprised. I had assumed Papa's backbone had been Ammiji or even Mama but no, it was Bhuaji always.

Bhagalpur Jail

Letter to Dilloo Bhua[6]

Besides various things, from the easternmost part of the country, young girls are to be married to unknown men in West Punjab. They are all in a cabin under the supervision of Balban Khan's accomplices. The guards have been bribed and the girls told not to talk to strangers; all is hush-hush in that cabin for the poor girls don't know what's in store for them. Whatever will be will be, some of them would sing if they'd ever heard of Doris Day. They'll never see their parents again. Balban says the parents are accomplices for they have nothing to feed these girls, and he's paid them well enough, he adds with a shrug of his shoulders. But what a pity, I say nevertheless. 'Now

[6] The first bit of the letter is missing

look here,' he says to me, 'be practical, can you see your children?' No, I say quietly. 'Well then,' he says, 'it's the same for them too, isn't it? They'll get used to it and settle down well enough. At least, in Pakistan they'll have enough to eat. In Bangladesh they starve.' I still don't appreciate his reasoning and he knows it. Clever Pathan. Well, that's Chagu din, he says as the train keeps perfect time and it's going to make it to the Bhagalpur platform at 8.25 a.m. sharp. What do you give him for carrying your cargo? I ask. 'Beef,' says Balban Khan. Chagu din loves beef and Balban's friendship. That's all he values, Balban says.

So the next time you're travelling by Teensukhia Mail and the diesel locomotive pulls in at 8.25 a.m., look towards its engine and you may get a glimpse of this dark, fat, and ugly man with a tiffin carrier in his hand. That will be Balban Khan with beef biryani or kebabs. Or both, with a flask. What's in the flask you'll want to know so I may as well tell you. It's Ganga Jal, from the Ganga which flows hard by the prison!

Don't mind the punctuation, missing words and so on as I have to keep chivy minding the eye of the prowling warders. Letters from jail aren't written on the best of bond and there's always a break in one's thoughts, because the chain in thought gets broken when you have to put away the letter for hours and sometimes days. In the Bharatpur jail I asked the superintendent, that horrible unctuous Upadhaya, to have my cell swept. He had a broom handed over to me and cheekily said, 'self-help is the best help'. He'd meant to humiliate me but I soon realized what a wise thing he'd repeated and since then I haven't asked for any personal chores to be done for me. I carry my own bucket of water, polish my own shoes, and if no one comes I clean my own cell. In Bharatpur, I washed my own clothes too though here the pania does the washing. So, statuswise I have risen since my Bharatpur days. Though if they give you one thing they always take away another. Here they've taken away my interviews with my family. So I'd rather wash my own clothes too.

My pania is a dacoit, but a very nice chap by the name of Mandal. Whenever he can he tells me stories about his land and his exploits.The latter, of course, I don't appreciate but do you know he does something wonderful and I don't know where he's learnt it from, for every morning when he sweeps and dusts and makes my bed, he sweetly places a fresh flower on my pillow below the counterpane. It's very touching. These days they have small marigolds in the prison, and since he can go anywhere he likes, that is, within the four walls of the Dachau, he picks a flower or plant and brings it in.

Bhenji, so these are the little gestures that keep one's morale up and keep one going. If you have any interesting newspaper clippings just put them in an envelope and leave them with the person from whom you collect this 'dak' and tell him to have it sent to me. You know you have kept me going and there were tough days when I could have taken it no longer; but for your inspiring talk, you would never have seen me with my chin up. I'm over the hump now and it's mainly due to you. So keep visiting me as often as you can.

I'm writing a little note for Hardev Singh, Mrs Nirlep Kaur's son, the heir to Sardar Bahadur Ranjit Singh's fortunes. If you think it will help, please give it to him. Hardev was in school with me in BCS before he went to Doon but much junior, I think he may remember me. Another person who was with me in school but much senior was Ruskin Bond. He lives in Mussoorie and writes occasionally for the *Indian Express.* I enjoy reading what he writes. When I was in Mussoorie for my training (police) I was amongst giants, meaning people with impressive doctorates and chaps from Oxford and Cambridge. I was a mere BA (Hons) from Punjab and amongst these fuddy-duddies I did feel a little tied down. But Ruskin Bond was very sweet and he would occasionally walk over from literally the other side of town for the sake of the old-school tie, and join me for lunch in the main dining room of Charlieville. The fuddy-duddies would die to be introduced, which I would obligingly do and I rose in their esteem! I wish you could write to him and request him to write more articles in the papers, for I do enjoy reading them. Perhaps if you wrote just Ruskin Bond, Mussoorie, on the envelope, he may receive the letter—being one of the old residents besides a renowned writer.

Well, Bhenji, I keep asking you to do this and that far too often and I'm apprehensive that one day you may say—who the devil do you think you are!

Till then I'll perhaps keep bothering you. I haven't revised the letter, it's impossible under the circumstances so excuse the errors. Give my love to the boys and Bhayaji who's given up tourism and taken up my case.

See you after you've received this, hopefully! I love you very very much . . .

Letter to Chhote Bhuaji

My case in Patna High Court was to be heard on 24 October but the C.J.[7] has been transferred. Let's see what happens.

I wonder how the Akali will fight the elections. Horicke,[8] the tyrant of East Germany, has resigned. Tyrants generally are on the retreat!

Javier Perez de Cuellar, the general secretary of the UN has been here in Delhi to receive the Nehru Peace Prize. Is he blind to the massacre of the Sikhs, raping of our women, detention without trial of thousands of Sikhs locked up without legal or medical aid? He is officially

[7] The presiding judge.

[8] Propably Erich Honecker, communist leader of East Germany, who resigned after the fall of the Berlin Wall.

designated to be the protector of civil liberties and human values enshrined in the Universal Declaration of Human Rights, yet he is blind even as the world celebrates the anniversary of the storming of the Bastille in 1789 and the centenary of the French Revolution, one of the greatest events in world history, which unleashed the glorious principles of life, liberty, and fraternity—what a shame! And what compounds the shame is that President Francois Mitterrrand of France, whose country's given so much for liberty, should also come here and decide to have himself blindfolded and remain gloriously ignorant of the genocide of the Sikh race, sanctioned by law and enshrined in the Constitution by virtue of the 59th Amendment!

Now what about Salman Rushdie, and all the brouhaha in the so-called liberal West and our press here? All right, he's written a book denouncing Islam, but they say he must be protected because freedom of speech is an article of faith.

Here am I, who has written to the government and the President of India complaining of the atrocities, the total destruction of our places of worship, and the plight of the Sikh people and the government not only dismisses me but charges me with sedition and waging a war against India, tortures me physically, humiliates me, keeps me in solitary confinement, dismisses a constitutionally elected assembly when I want to contest an election, denies me a trial, keeps me in jail for four and a half years now, and not a whisper in protest from the so-called guardians of the world conscience, all of whom are expressing such outrage at the threat to Rushdie's life?

It's not that I don't support them and agree with them absolutely that what he's done certainly does not warrant the death penalty, but what piques me is their very hypocrisy. Not one of them has raised their little finger in my case and tried to protect my Right of Free Expression!

Heard over the radio that Jathedar Talwandi has called a meeting on 16 March 1989 at Amritsar so that he can bring about unity in the Akali Dal. Jathedar Tota Singh has said that J. Talwandi has no such powers to summon any such meeting. So I think that it's become a controversial issue right at the onset. I don't know much about Talwandi's character but the little I do is that he's a very shallow man. As president of the Akali Dal in 1980, he brought down his own ministry led by Sardar Badal and that, too, in league with Sanjay Gandhi and preferred central rule to Akali rule. Can you picture a greater fool? The man has no self-respect pride or honour. Once he brought the Centre in, our troubles started and no Sikh has rested in peace since then. Blue Star, Woodrose,[9] Black

[9] Comprised rounding up thousands of supposed Sikh militants, and aimed at eradicating separatist groups in Punjab, after Blue Star. An estimated 8000 youths went missing as a result of these operations carried out by the army.

Thunder Parts I and II, the assassination of Sant Longowal and God knows what else in the future!

After he had his own ministry dismissed, he bargained for a Rajya Sabha seat and gave up the presidentship to Longowal. Immediately after that deal, he went back upon his word and founded his own parallel Akali Dal, which I know was supported by the Centre. He then began the morcha for the Anandpur Sahib Resolution.

And while he was president of the Akali Dal, he played Rip Van Winkle with the Resolution and because this morcha of his had no support he went one step further than Sant Longowal and began advocating Khalistan. And now if I believe what I heard over the radio—I heard it said that Jathedar Talwandi advocates full allegiance to the Constitution and believes in the integrity of the country! There's a lovely joke explaining the conduct of Jathedar Talwandi which Virji Manjit[10] once told me, but since you're a lady and my sister I shan't narrate it.

Letter to Mama

My darling Geeta,

I have been very well since you last met me. They were to produce me before a magistrate on 27 April 1989, but

[10] Papa's elder brother.

didn't. What happened?

It's getting warmer. I shut the windows opening into the western court to keep out the loo and the dust; the windows opening into the verandah, I shut too, but not totally as then there would be no light and the warders wouldn't be able to see me. Generally, they leave me in peace unless an officer troubles them to patrol, which they do wearing their jack boots which go thak-thak-thak, like the Thakkar Report,[11] which is a nightmare for Dhawan[12] and the government.

Now I'll tell you a little family history as has been told to me. My great ancestor General Budh Singh, founder of our family's fortunes, had four wives. The practice of sati had crept up amongst the Sikhs, because of the influence of Hinduism. Since our family came from Jaisalmer in Rajasthan and settled in Sheikhupura district (now in Pakistan), the Rajput background could also not be discounted. So when General Budh Singh died, the youngest of his wives said she'd mount the pyre with him and immolate herself with her husband.

It must be said that it was entirely voluntary for the other three wives had no such desire to immolate themselves. She bedecked herself in her bridal finery, climbed the pyre, and took her husband's head in her

---

[11] The report of the Commission of Inquiry into the assassination of Prime Minister Indira Gandhi by Justice Thakkar.

[12] R.K. Dhawan, former presonal secretary to Mrs Gandhi.

lap, when all at once the general's relatives unsheathed their swords. She was livid with rage and told them she was no coward and would not move an inch. 'Look here,' she said, 'I have loved my lord and master and dutifully I'm going with him. You wretched cowards, sheathe your daggers or my curse will be upon you.' And like lambs they did her bidding. The pyre was lit and she immolated herself. It was a barbaric custom, and the Singh Sabha movement put an end to it as did the British, who vowed to confiscate the lands of Sikh sardars if they practised sati or child infanticide. The sardars loved their land and the Singh Sabha movement also had a strong moral effect.

For your information, the Jalla Sardars were great defaulters like my family in this evil practice. What bedevils us is dowry deaths, which pain me so much. Why are girls coerced to bring money once they are married? I find it so distasteful and evil. I'm glad that in my family we don't look for a dowry directly or subtly, and my brother's two marriages and mine will bear this out.

Now I'll tell you about my grandmother's family from my father's side. My grandfather had four wives. Two were sisters from Khamano, and of the younger of these two, Dad was born. His mother died before I was born but his aunt/mother was Wade Maaji who gave me a lot of love. She ran the kitchen till she could manage it.

She had another sister who was married in Attari but to a lesser gentleman and so she always carried a chip on her shoulder.

After her husband died, she came to live with us. She was addressed as Maaji Attariwale. Because Wade Maaji was the most well off, many of her relatives and widowed cousins came to live with her from time to time. One of them was Maaji Hindustanwale—please ask Bibiji who this Maaji was and where exactly she came from.

Maaji Hindustanwale came from somewhere in UP or Bihar—anyone who lived beyond the Jamuna came from Hindustan, as simple as that, at least that was what we were told when we were children. She was fair and plump and she wore a sari, with her tummy popping out of her blouse, which amazed me because I had never seen a woman who didn't completely cover her body with clothes. She was forever chewing betel leaves and Bibiji would daily in her hisaab-kitaab note down the betel leaves that had come for her. Bibiji then maintained the hisaab-kitaab and the staff doing the bazaar had to give her a daily account. Imagine Bibiji keeping hisaab and bound down to a budget!!

I could never feel at ease with Maaji Hindustanwale because of her unconventional dress, her speech in Hindi, and her chewing betel leaf. She would cuddle me in her lovely soft belly and tell me stories of elephants and tigers, both of which she'd seen. Wade Maaji kept a careful eye on me and one day when just the two of us were alone she asked me why I didn't like her sister, and without waiting for my answer she said she knew it was because her sister wore peculiar clothes and spoke a different language. She said that when I grew up and travelled I'd find most women were like her because India was a big country and most women dressed like her. Wade Maaji was widely travelled and regularly went on tirath yatra, to the Kumbh Mela, etc. But she added that she knew that even though I didn't love her sister, she'd noticed that I gave her due respect and she said that was enough for her. And that she was satisfied as long as I always showed respect to people. She gave me a lovely hug, an endearing one. She taught me to do the Japji Sahib and I would do it because I loved her dearly. If I didn't eat she would never get annoyed but get so hurt that she'd begin to sob and when she sobbed, red rings would form around her eyes and since Dads visited her mornings and evenings I would be afraid he'd notice the red eyes and enquire and so I would quickly eat before she began to sob. Of course, she wouldn't ever have tattled on me to Dads—he would find out from the staff and woe betide the person who had brought her to such a state. For a very long time I didn't know Wade Maaji wasn't his mother. She died in 1967 when I was under training at Mount Abu and Dads wrote that I needn't come for the bhog. I was very angry because her bhog wasn't considered important enough for me to attend. But then Dads are Dads! And one can never question them. Sometimes even here in this Dachau I miss her terribly.

With lots and lots of love, my darling, I love you most of all, your FE.

Letter to Mama

Darling GI,[13]

I write this while being driven to the courts in handcuffs. I have not been allowed to write to you all since July. Your letters written in July and August were received on September 1986. Bibiji brought your letter but when I began to read it, it was snatched away and I don't know when it will be given to me by the superintendent.

You are superb and I love you very much. The children have grown, I have missed three of their birthdays. Give my love to Emaan and my prayers and good wishes for his birthday. It will be Nanki's birthday after Emaan's—give her my love—and then Pavit's. Give her my love. I can't write to them. Please make them understand. I love them all very much and you have brought them up so well, singlehanded, and attended to my case as well.

I'm approaching the courts.

[13] Geetinder, Mama's name.

With lots of love
yours FE Sims
P.S. no dental treatment, no religious service

Still in solitary confinement (this is the worst). Now I'm locked in even during the day. The jail superintendent hasn't implemented any of the court orders. Please speak to Mr Jethmalani.

Letter from Emaan to Papa

Chandigarh
August 1985

My dearest Papa,

How are you? Have the authorities had your tooth filled or is it still paining? I hope they have.We worry about you a lot and wish that you were back. Bhavani Bhen's party went off very well. Nearly all her class girls came and three of her class boys too. We danced and had a very delicious party, with cake, rasgullas, samosas and cucumber sandwiches. But the very next day she had fever. Even Hari Vir and Bhagad Singh had fever.

This time when Neeti Masi went abroad she got me a pair of trekking and snow shoes. They are green and made by Scarpa. She bought them in England.

Our exams are starting on the 3rd and ending on the 6th, my birthday. Mama is getting me a pair of black trousers and shoes for my birthday which will also be used for Jaya Bhen's wedding.

Papa, how do you like my sketch? I made every inch of it and nobody helped me, not even the family artist, Pavit.

The weather over here is hot and humid. There are a lot of mosquitoes around, I suppose that is the reason why everybody is getting fever.

In this school we have mid-terms too and I am going to Saach Pass with two of my other friends but as yet the shadow of the exams looms ahead because our mid-terms are starting on the 19th of next month.

Our inter-house football matches have started today and our house won both matches.

More news next time. Till then bye with tons of love, kisses, hugs.

Your loving son,

Emaan

P.S. I am writing with a Parker.

Letter from Papa to me

Dachau Bharatpur
18 November 1985

Darling Pavit,

Sat Sri Akal. Thank you very much for your loving letters and your 'rakhri'. When am I coming home? Well, that's a million-dollar question. I don't know, darling, but as soon as Rajiv Gandhi feels that Sikhs could be set at liberty, I trust that the Dachau gates will be opened. Until then, you know that I have been sentenced to two years' imprisonment without a trial. The term will expire in December 1986 and so I trust I will be in prison till then. But don't worry, I'm quite well and I look after myself despite the harsh conditions. Yesterday I started getting my ration of 20 gm of cooking oil (mustard). For the last ten months the authorities have been giving me only one square meal a day, and no oil. Can you imagine cooking a meal with just 20 gm of oil?

Yesterday was a good day; the doctor of the jail has sanctioned me one pau of green vegetables a day. That will be a good change, I've barely eaten a green vegetable these last ten months. Often enough, there are a number of weevils in my porridge, horrible white-looking insects with orange noses. I gently pick them out and eat the porridge as I have to keep my strength.

No, darling, I haven't begun painting as I never have the time. Most of my time is taken up by prayers and meditation and then I have to attend to my daily chores, all household duties.

Would you like me to send the art books back so that they could be of use to you? I don't think I really will use these books. Perhaps I may send them back?

You write very well and your handwriting is superb. I'm so proud that you're doing so well. If you look up 'Art' in the *Encyclopaedia Britannica* you will enrich your knowledge. Ask your Taiji to buy you some books on the history of art and lives of some famous painters. Art, as you know, is as old as history and primitive man painted scenes on the walls of caves. Paints were then made from juices of plants and herbs—it's a very interesting subject and since you want to be an artist, perhaps it would be good to begin studying the subject right now.

The greatest Sikh artist of this century was Amrita Shergill. She's a relative of your mother's and was a friend of your Ammiji. And when your Ammiji and Amrita Shergill were little girls about your age, the latter nearly tickled your Ammiji into a state of unconsciousness in Simla. Ask Ammiji—it's a pretty interesting anecdote.

So I do think we have artist blood in our veins and I think if you seriously study the subject, you may become a very famous artist in your own right. Of course, if you do well you could go to Paris. However, do ask your Taiji about the history of art and do begin to study the subject. In fact, there's no dearth of material in our own library and your Mama also knows a lot.

My cell and its enclosure are very dull. The prison authorities have very kindly allowed me to put down some flower saplings. As such I have quite a number of marigold plants and they do cheer me up whenever I walk about my enclosure. But since this letter will be censored I might find all the plants uprooted one day because I've written and told you that the flowers made my life more bearable. The authorities don't like anything that may make my life pleasant. Their rule is that of the seventeenth-century Puritans, who it is said hated bear-baiting not because it gave pain to the bear but because it gave pleasure to the spectators! They banned bear-baiting on this account.

How are Nikki and the gorkha?[14] I hope you look after them both. And how's your dog? Write and tell me though you don't like him very much.

How's Pavan Bhen and her baby? Please find out all the news about her and write to me as I'm most anxious to know about her.

Look after yourself. Be polite and courteous and considerate of others and you'll grow up to be a great lady.

With pots and pots of love,

Your loving Papa

---

[14] The domestic help's children.

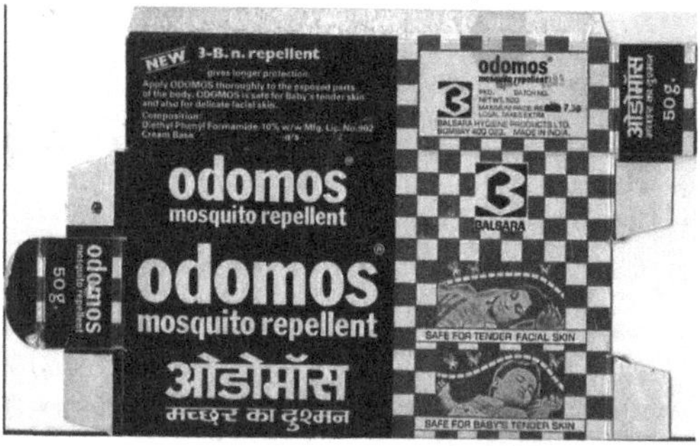

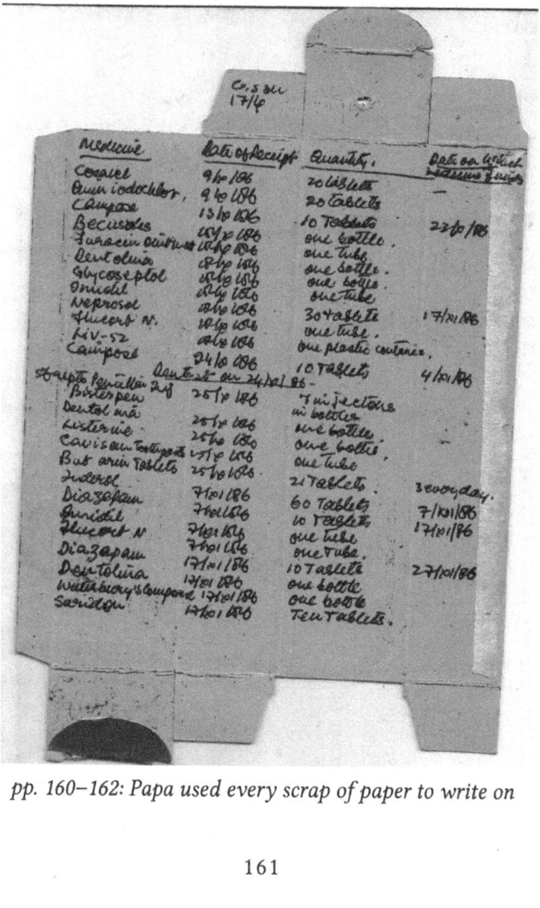

pp. 160–162: Papa used every scrap of paper to write on

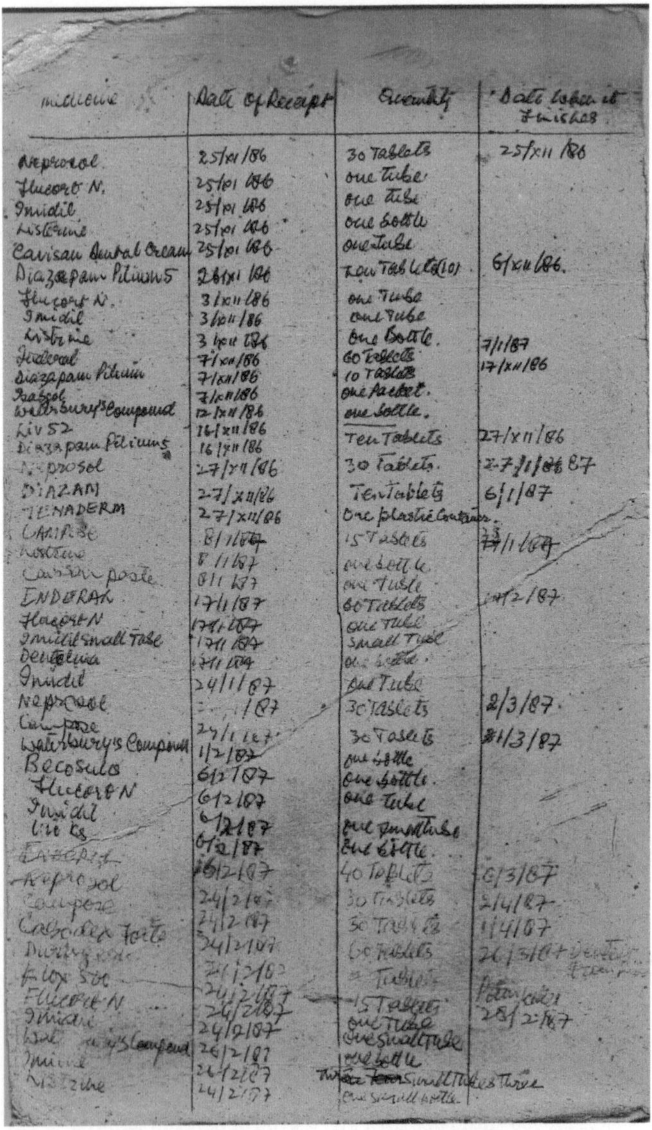

Medicine	Date of Receipt	Quantity	Date taken & Finishes
Neprosol	25/XI/86	30 Tablets	25/XI/86
Flucort N.	25/XI/86	one tube	
Imidil	25/XI/86	one tube	
Listerine	25/XI/86	one bottle	
Cavisan Dental Cream	25/XI/86	one tube	
Diazepam Pilium 5	26/XI/86	ten Tablets (10)	6/XII/86.
Flucort N.	3/XII/86	one Tube	
Imidil	3/XII/86	one Tube	
Listerine	3/XII/86	One Bottle.	7/1/87
Inderal	7/XII/86	60 Tablets	17/XII/86
Diazapam Pilium	7/XII/86	10 Tablets	
Isabgol	7/XII/86	one Packet.	
Waterbury's Compound	12/XII/86	one bottle.	
Liv 52	16/XII/86		
Diazapam Pilium 5	16/XII/86	Ten Tablets	27/XII/86
Neprosol	27/XII/86	30 Tablets.	27/1/~~86~~ 87
DIAZAM	27/XII/86	Ten Tablets	6/1/87
TENADERM	27/XII/86	One plastic Container.	
CARIPASE	8/1/87	15 Tablets	23/1/87
Listerine	8/1/87	one bottle	
Cavisan paste	8/1/87	one Tube	
ENDERAL	17/1/87	60 Tablets	14/2/87
Flucort N	17/1/87	one Tube	
Imidil small Tube	17/1/87	small Tube	
Dentelina	17/1/87	one bottle.	
Imidil	24/1/87	one Tube	
Neprosol	[illegible]/87	30 Tablets	2/3/87.
Compose	24/1/87	30 Tablets	31/3/87
Waterbury's Compound	1/2/87	one bottle	
Becosules	6/2/87	one bottle.	
Flucort N	6/2/87	one Tube	
Imidil	6/2/87	one small tube	
Liv 52	6/2/87	one bottle.	
~~Enderal~~	16/2/87	40 Tablets	6/3/87
Neprosol	24/2/87	30 Tablets	2/4/87
Compose	24/2/87	30 Tablets	1/4/87
Calcidex Forte	24/2/87	60 Tablets	26/3/87 [illegible]
[illegible]	24/2/87	[illegible] Tablets	
Flox 500	24/2/87	15 Tablets	[illegible] 28/2/87
Flucort N	24/2/87	one Tube	
Imidil	24/2/87	one small Tube	
Waterbury's Compound	26/2/87	one bottle	
Imidil	26/2/87	~~Three Four~~ small Tubes Three	
Listerine	24/2/87	one small bottle.	

White as new...again and again
POWER PACKED
Surf
washes whitest...
keeps clothes like new!
How fresh, how white a new shirt looks in its box!... With Surf, it will stay white-as-new. Wash after wash.
Because Surf's ingredients are the most active, most protecting. To lift out stubborn dirt and preserve the whiteness. Yet protect the fabric's newness!... There may be hundreds of washing powders, but only one you can trust: Only Surf makes sure your whites and coloureds stay whitest and brightest—just like new!
Fresh New Perfume
And now anything washed in New Power Packed Surf is so nice to be near to! Because Surf's new perfume makes all your clothes smell so nice'n clean!
NEW
Power Packed Surf washes whitest...
keeps clothes like new!
DETERGENT POWDER.
MFD. BY HINDUSTAN LEVER LTD. BOMBAY 400 020
WHEN PACKED NET WT. 1.5 kg.

My dearest cousin Dilloo Bhanji, As a prisoner of Gandhi's for the last four years, living in solitary confinement, one has moments of joy and they come in various forms. So I'll share my moments of joy with you. Firstly it's a great moment in history that the hated Russians have retreated after nine years of occupation of Afghanistan. One out of every twelve Afghans were died to expel these rogues who went out of their way to support, along with the Vietnamese, the destruction and desecration of the Golden Temple in 1984. I am specially joyous since in one of my official communications to Government in 1979 I had analysed and ~~practiced~~ predicted the occupation of Afghanistan by the Russians. The second moment of joy has been that they gave me the Readers Digest Dictionary you had brought. I thought they wouldn't give me the book as it had maps and had words like Sachan, which is anathema to them, in it. So what I do is look up every country, its map and latitude in the book, whenever that country is in the news. Since my view of the world has broadened as I love to see the latitude and the country I feel less claustrophobic. So you see what a wonderful thing you have done. Bibiji was looking so lovely and fresh and so full of ideas that I found her [illegible] which was again joyful. My garden is a riot of colour and the people, the warders, the prisoners and the official love visiting it and some of them risk far too much just to have a peep for it's a very high security area and no one is allowed except on special business. Sardar Ranjit Singh Brahmpura was here to see me. He wanted me to appoint Baba Joginder Singh as the acting President. I said he was already the acting President. He said he nevertheless needed my formal approval. I told him that could be decided by the members of the Presidium and the accent of the [illegible]. Some people from the [illegible] like Harminder Singh, Darshan Singh would be coming to see me in the Jail, the same people who came to see me earlier through Satish Sharma. I don't know what they'll want but the same thing as previously i.e. to make Babaji the Acting President. The Centre [illegible] sent to revive their dialogue with this camp after it was a disgrace with Operation Black Thunder. What's their image in the country side? If anything happens I will inform Daddy Bhapaji and Bibiji. They are keeping my head on the block and negotiating with me by threatening me with another case. You see Dilloo Bhanji it's like this. If I succumb to this sort of immoral pressure and am let out I won't be able to live with my conscience and on the other side I see more torture and prolonged incarceration. With the grace of God and the moral help you and Bibiji have given me I have decided to live with my conscience and not accept the easy way. If Gandhiji is going to torture and kill me I am prepared for it. Lets see what will happen. The Sikh leaders would like to see me gone but I don't see what they will gain by this as the people will never accept them i.e if they succeed. Sardar Barnala was to see me as per CSB report but he never came. He's very unpopular with the Sikh masses — that's what I know. I may be wrong. You must be frightfully busy and I wish you well in the service of the Khalsa Panth. But do [illegible] and have the Leaders begin courting arrest. Tell them it would be difficult to give [illegible] With lots and lots of love. Your

Letter from Papa to Emaan

Dachau Bhagalpur
3 February 1987

Darling Emaan, thank you very much for your loving letter. I'm glad you're doing well in studies and outdoor activities. Keep it up. I heard you had a splendid time in the pind. Scooter riding and the rest! Jolly good. How are our cows? Does anyone look after them?

There's a change in the weather here and the sun has begun to beat down hard. Soon the summer will come.

I had a team of very senior doctors come to examine me. They took my ECG, probed my heart, pierced their fingers into my gut, and finally pronounced me fit and said I was in good health. That was a pleasing verdict for I haven't had a very good verdict in my favour for a long time. My tooth may also receive dental care as the dentist was here the other day and said he'd have to get the molar X-rayed before proceeding further. That may not mean very much but at least it's a few paces forward. Then I believe that the letters I receive from you all will be delivered faster. So you see all these are signs that things are improving.

On Republic Day, the authorities very kindly gave me a few jalebees which I relished very much. And Mr Chaudhary, the jail superintendent, came to look me up and fortunate it was, for he hurriedly had my lunch cooked as there was no cook and a new one had to be brought. Unfortunately, they didn't associate me with the flag unfurling ceremonies. That's because I'm not allowed out of my enclosure and they couldn't have possibly arranged a special ceremony in my ward. So since I had nothing to do the whole morning save eat jalebees, the visit of the superintendent was significant for I got some food or else on Republic Day I would have simply starved. Unlike you, I don't squirrel away any food and save for a rainy day. Must learn to do so. I remember how, as a child, you used to hide some chapattis under your mattress for a midnight feast or for that matter when we were out on a shikaar. When everyone had nothing to eat you would take out your food packet, carefully preserved in a polythene bag, and eat, with all the others looking on. You certainly learnt early in life how to preserve yourself.

Anyway I thank the superintendent for feeding me on 26 January 1987. The girls have been writing to me complaining that you tease and worry them too much. What exactly do you do to annoy them, because in front of me you are like a lamb and it would appear butter wouldn't melt in your mouth? I just can't believe that you can be the cause of so much annoyance. Perhaps they can't take a joke! Make them read Wodehouse and Harriet and perhaps they'll mellow down.

Well here we come to the end and I'll say the usual—say your prayers, look after Mama and the girls and Bapuji and Ammiji and do write to me more often.

With lots and lots of love. I love you very much.

Your loving papa

Letter to Papa from Emaan

20 February 1989

Dear Papa,

How are we? I am writing from Chandigarh but will be back in Sanawar this evening slogging away up and down the hillside, but it won't be that bad this term because we'll be the seniormost class in the dorms and we will be running the school as captains, prefects, etc. because the present upper sixers will be preparing for their board exams. I have been golfing every day and am playing to about 20. I haven't started using the woods yet but I will next hols. Papa, your woods fibreglass has rotted so a new one has to be put into them otherwise the set is fine. Cleo has been fine and I've been neglecting her for some time but I made up for that by taking her for golf practice in the leisure valley. She retrieves the balls very well but gets tired of getting them after some time.

Girimere Vir's exams have come up so he's been nabbed by Taiji and Mama and has to study. Nanki

Kaur has been having headaches which turned out to be migraines, but have got much better now. She's taking some biochemical salts for it. Pavit Kaur is busy with school and doesn't have time for much else except for a nasty word here and there. This time I haven't been for any shikar or fishing, which is sad because I love to fish.

This evening when I get to school all the prefects will be announced and one of my best friends has chances of becoming school prefect or M.I. prefect, two of the seniormost positions in school.

I think I will end now.

More news from school.

Love

Emaan

Letter to me from Papa

April 1989

The Dachau

My darling Pavit,

I hope you are well. I haven't seen you for over a year perhaps, so do come to Dachau Tihar. It was lovely seeing Mama. She cheered me up immensely because otherwise in solitary confinement and more false accusations one is bound not to have one's chin up.

I don't do much because it's hot and windy. I listen to good classical music on the BBC and if you want to listen to Chopin do tune into BBC on Sundays at 7.15 a.m. or Tuesdays at 8.15 p.m.

I believe the French orchestra played Chopin in Chandigarh. In the new charge sheet you will hear that besides writing to Amnesty International, I used to attend music classes. How that makes me seditious in character, God only knows. I think the Gandhis are going loony.

Do write a long full of 'gups'[15] letter. I love you very, very much and miss you too.

With lots and lots of love,

Your loving Papa

Letter to Nanki from Papa

Dachau Bhagalpur April 1989

My darling Nanki,

I hope your migraines are better. They can tie one down so badly.

Dilloo Bhenji said she was about your age when she

[15] Gossip

began getting them. I have migraines too but they're not as severe as yours and only last a few hours.

When are you going to come and see me? It's been ages since we met and you must come soon. There is no electricity today and it's very hot. My tooth also aches and I have sent a message to the doctor but no one has come so far. The mango trees are overladen with fruit and the monkeys invite themselves over. I have a catapult, for that's the only thing that scares them and so we have managed to save some fruit. We make mango chutney every day and it's quite nice. I eat very little during the day as it's too hot and the appetite is not so good.

Well, do read a lot and I promise you your horse.

I love you very, very much.

With lots of love,

Your loving Papa

Letter to Emaan from Papa

Dachau, Bhagalpur

Darling Emaan,

Mama's here and she's told me about your quest for a Rolex. You are a natty little chap, and I haven't stopped laughing since your Mama told me that three days ago. You know I still don't have a Rolex and how are you going to get one? And in school? They'll steal it away in no time. I have a beautiful, steel winding Omega and I had a mind to offer it to you but since you love a Rolex more and since I don't have one I'm sorry I can't oblige. Maybe if you chase around Bapuji and Ammiji, you may succeed or if you help me out of the Dachau—I'll present you one as a thanksgiving!

Best of luck anyway and I'm most amused. Next you'll be preferring a Rolls to a Jaguar and only if you go to Exeter, sonny bunny, and become a Nobel-winning scientist you'll have your Rolls and I'll be very very proud. You can drive your ol' man and his wife sometimes.

I love you very very much.

Lots of love from Papa

Bihar, Bhagalpur Prison

Cloudy weather with a drizzle. Read the *Indian Express*, the *Times of India* and the *Hindustan Times*. BBC says that the Indian troops massacred some fifty Tamils in Sri Lanka in retaliation for six Indian soldiers who were ambushed. The Tamils were made to face down and shot dead in the head. There were women and children too. This happened on 2 August and the news was suppressed by the Indians since then. I felt sick and horrible. Late at night I began having a migraine. It rained cats and dogs in the early hours. I took a painkiller at 4 a.m. for my migraine, but when I woke up at 6.30 it hadn't subsided or disappeared. Read *HT, TOI, IE* and the *Sunday Mail.* Dr Deo came to see me and told me that the authorities are a worried lot and that they're making all-out efforts to produce me in the Delhi Court on 19 June.

The jailor came and I told him about Too-too, the bearer, and how he'd disappeared and never stayed here. Everyone has gone to see the Mahabharata. It's all very quiet. I had a Sunday lunch of poori alu. Re-read all the papers. Migraine's still there.

14 August 1989

Dr Om Prakash Aggarwal came and said my scrotum was loose, so in the evening a surgeon came to check me. The surgeon wanted to examine me for prostate but hadn't thought to bring along his gloves and the prison didn't have any. An eye specialist had come along too and he said my eyes were NORMAL! It's that bad.

15 August 1989

Heard Rajiv's Independence Day address. He abused his opponents, said they were reactionaries, traitors, communalists, hand-in-glove with his mother's assassins, etc. etc.

P.W. Botha, the evil man, has resigned, and a somewhat better man, De Klerk, has replaced him in South Africa. Read the *HT*, *TOI*, *IE* and *SM*. The Superintendent came and offered me a plate of sweetmeats (it being Independence Day), but as I didn't feel free or independent, I politely refused the offering. Went to bed feeling low.

16 August 1989

Woke up to find that my transistor is not catching any station on short wave. I am miserable for this is one of the rare pleasures I'm provided with in my strict incarceration. I had it sent to the jailor for repairs.

17 August 1939

COURT

Bibiji, G.I and Teddyji were there. Judge Verma said in his judgement that Attinderpal would not be tried but Sukhtaj would. Court was adjourned.

Spent a few precious moments with my mother, wife, and brother-in-law. In the evening I was flown out to Delhi and later in the evening produced before the chief magistrate, Khanna, who said I'd be given upper division class I treatment as in Bihar and allowed my radio.

At Tihar I went into the same cell as the time before. They have increased the height of the stone wall of my perimeter!

18 August 1989

I spent the day in my Tihar Jail compound. I was given the *Indian Express* and the *Hindustan Times* but not the *TOI* or *SM.* Gupta, the deputy superintendent, and Surinder Mohan came in and Dutta was with them. In the evening Dr Wadhera came to see me.

I have a splitting headache, it's 11 p.m. I sent for the prison doctor but he came only the following day at 8 a.m.

19 August 1989

Court in the secret-trial room.

I was happy to see Mr Jethmalani, Dilloo Bhenji, and Sodhi there. R.S Sodhi put up a draft to the Chief Justice, the Supreme Court, which I signed, and before I could say Jack Robinson I saw Dilloo Bhenji and Sodhi race off with it to the Supreme Court.

Met H.H, Neeti, Bhayaji Prithpal, Inderjit Bhenji, GI, Bibiji, and Dads. Dr Wadhera very sweetly brought me a three-band Philips radio, had it passed by Mr Khanna who also passed three books, all of which I was given. I was very happy.

11 October 1989

It's a pleasant day and clouds are gathering. They are travelling in the northwest direction. I have had the rose, the only one of five that survived, uprooted and transplanted in a sunnier spot. I am having the roots aired and I pruned one unhealthy branch. I didn't receive my paper at all. No *TOI*, *HT*, *SM*, or *IE*.

I had some brinjals and tomato saplings put down. There was a brief spell of rain after I was locked in.

12 October 1989

Read IE of the 10th, 11th and 12th, *SM* of 11th and 12th, *HT* of 11th and 12th and the *TOI* of the 11th and 12th. It's a clear blue sky. I put down sixteen gladioli bulbs on 12 September. Today I noticed that the last of the lot had popped. Damn good results!

Too-too, the bearer, is malingering and says he's ill. As a result, the entire routine falls into disarray, the day he decides to sham!

I have had no proper vegetables. The tomato sauce hasn't arrived. Pretty bad management, and I told Mr Dubey the jailor so. He said he'd put everything in order.

13 October 1989

This morning at 3.30 a.m. fat Pandey, the assistant jailor, came on duty. He's a boisterous chap and talks very loudly. So I plugged the earplugs (given by Dilloo Bhenji) into my ears and went back to sleep.

The bade jamadar came and said that Too-too is sick and in hospital so he sent Sitaram who will look after the garden and Mukhia becomes my bearer. Read *HT*, *TOI* and *SM* no *IE*.

14 October 1989

It's a good sunny day but bound to be warm. A warder who has some knowledge of plants came to see my gladioli. Most of them have begun to droop and look very sad and ill. He said he'd spray something today and that they'd recover. He'd spray the chrysanthemums too.

Dilloo Bhenji and Geeta came to see me. Very sweet and bold of them, for they came all alone. The jailor allowed me a verbal interview. GI was looking well. The mountain air has done her wonders!

15 October 1989

They came and sprayed my plants. It's a sunny day and last night was warm. I had the fan on. The Bofors scandal is on full blast and Gandhi had to adjourn Parliament. G.I. told me that the home secretary, Patna, had issued orders for my dental check up, TV etc. When I asked the jailor whether he'd received the order, he said he hadn't. But the good doctor came and told me that the orders had been received four days ago.

Read *TOI*, *SM* and *IE*.

I have a bad migraine. Missed the BBC programme 'Letter from America' on the radio by Alistair Cooks.

16 October 1989

The migraine continued all of last night and today. I spent the day in bed. It was very painful. I steamed my face with Vicks fumes and that made me feel a wee bit better.

I didn't read at all or recite the Sukhmani Sahib or walk and say the Chaupais. It was a bad day.

17 October 1989

Gandhi has announced Parliamentary elections for 22nd and 24th November. I was much heartened.

18 October 1989

Last night was chilly, so I switched off the fan.

During this time, Papa was being ferried back and forth from New Delhi Tihar Jail and then back to Bhagalpur prison for his trial for the conspiracy to murder Indira Gandhi, which was being conducted in a special court at Tihar.

In October, while he was languishing in Bhagalpur Jail, the worst Hindu–Muslim violence in independent India broke out in Bhagalpur. Over 1000 people (around 900 of which were Muslims) were supposedly killed and around 50,000 were displaced from their homes. Papa in his diary gives a blow by blow account of the riots based on whispered snippets and news he got from his warders and his little factotum in prison . . .

27 October 1989

The riots in Bhagalpur

All of last night I heard bombs bursting and cries from nearby localities. The situation isn't under control, contrary to what the Centre's claiming, and the riots are spreading to nearby Munger. It's a dangerous situation. There's no sane hand, no moral voice to stop them if the crisis turns into a cataclysm.

Kalam, a Muslim warder, informed me that the Muslims are well prepared and that they have given as good as they receive. This may be true but when the riots gather momentum and spread, it will be a cakewalk for the Hindus. The Muslims look scared no doubt and though they are putting up a brave front, they know their Achilles' heel.

Jha is an old warder here and his son was in a hostel in the Muslim quarter of the city. After the Bhagalpur riots began, the son couldn't be found for two days. They'd all given him up for lost because they say the Muslims in their area had cut up the Hindus into little pieces. However, this morning I heard that the young man had surrendered himself to a police patrol, spent two days under their custody, and a police jeep brought him here this morning. A close shave! Thank God! The old warder would have died of grief. His son is the apple of his eye and he's invested every spare penny on his education.

I have had DDT sprayed on the chrysanthemums and have had the flower pots filled with fresh earth and farmyard manure. Lovely compost I had dug from my own yard, of rotted leaves and stems, which I had had thrown near the bogs and allowed to rot for a year. Compost of a dark, thick, and velvety texture ought to be good.

In the evening, the Hindi BBC broadcast announced that the superintendent, Ashok Kumar Divedi, had been transferred and Ram Iqbal Singh, the warder, said that Jha, the district magistrate (DM), had been transferred too and Ashok Kumar Singh had come in his place. Ram Iqbal Singh told me with much relish and excitement that the new DM was a strong Rajput officer and had shot dead several Muslims when posted at Gaya. There is popular support for superintendent Divedi, too, amongst the Hindus and they say that he'd shot down a leading Muslim leader. They love officers in direct proportion to the number of Muslims they shoot! The 200-odd Muslim prisoners brought to the prison have been put into a separate ward. They complain of brutality and seek medical aid.

Warder Pathak told me they listen to their complaints but don't inform the medical officer. Communal feelings against the Muslims are rising here in the jail and even Mukhia, my bearer, wants to kill a few. It's turning to madness, the hatred against the Muslims. Nath Thakur, the clerk tells me to wait till 9 November 1989, the day when the foundation stone for Lord Rama's temple will be laid in Ayodhya, and then watch the drama he says. I am watching from the ringside, an impartial observer, while both factions are telling me what's happening and how they feel. The CRP contingent here isn't impartial either, they've been out in the Muslim area and have been shooting Muslims. There is a Muslim constable with them and they say he shuts his eyes when they go hunting! Yesterday these men (CRP) had the contractor's godown opened and took sackfuls of potatoes. The contractor was trembling with fear and allowed them to take what they wanted. There is no resistance from the populace. They are terrified and live in absolute dread and fear, both of the armed forces and their rival communities.

28 October 1989

Last night I slept in relative peace. There were fewer bomb blasts and presumably with the induction of more troops, the authorities have managed to gain some control.

Today is an important cricket match between India and Pakistan at Eden Grounds, Calcutta. If India loses and the Muslims celebrate, that'll ignite fresh communal trouble. And yes it will be just as bad if Pakistan loses. For great national pride is involved.

Rajiv Gandhi never realized what he was doing in 1984 when he allowed the massacre of the Sikhs. He set a precedent and now he pays with the consequences. When in the government one mustn't ever allow communal feelings to raise their ugly head; they should be nipped in the bud quickly. But he played with fire and now he faces the Big Bang! I certainly wouldn't like to be in his shoes at this moment.

The BBC continues to report that things are totally out of control here in Bhagalpur. Yesterday, the jailor and the doctor came to see me after I was locked in, and they apologized for not sending me green veggies and fruit. I said I understood, for my stomach won't be able to take in anything, what with the whole town littered with corpses.

Thank God Geeta brought me a packet of cornflakes. I eat these for breakfast, with milk, of which there is no dearth as there are plenty of cows here. They have sent me some green veggies today from the prison farm.

'Neenooa' is what they call this vegetable and I never eat it but now I must as there is nothing else.

The barber, the new chap, a good man, has braved all odds and walked the sidetracks, avoiding Muslim habitations and security forces patrols to come and cut my nails. He tells me that all shops belonging to Muslims in Fatehpur basti, where he lives, have been looted but fortunately so far, there has been no loss of life. His little child is ill, but there's no medicine to be had or a doctor in sight. I could give him nothing, as he was accompanied by a warder who kept him well in sight lest we exchange anything.

I am sitting in the garden this morning and listening to the commentary for the cricket match between India and Pakistan. The garden is looking magnificent with the green grass and maroon flowers of the lovely tall coxcomb plant, with butterflies hovering over them, and birds twittering. It's ideal.

I have had the winter flower seeds put in and I hope I have a good nursery. It's the season of the green grasshoppers. Hundreds of them. I see crows and mynahs catching them in their beaks. The grasshoppers don't rest at night and they invade my room too. They're a nuisance for they get into the clothes and food, though the lizards slyly lie in wait and they make a good meal for them.

Pakistan have scored handsomely and built up a total of 279 runs in fifty overs.

Warder Pathak, the elderly man, says that the curfew has been relaxed till 3 p.m. and some shops in the town have even opened. Nate Khan is a senior warder here. He wears a long beard and is a devout Muslim. Shakaldev Singh is a stocky, short-statured Rajput who retired recently from the jail. He was good to me and keeps in touch. He was travelling down the left bank of the river to reach this place, through a ghat as the other route was blocked. En route he ran into Nate Khan and they both travelled together. As they reached the ghat on the opposite bank of the Ganga, from where they would cross over, a band of Hindu fanatics were chopping off the heads of Muslims. Shakaldev Singh asked them to stop but they told him to mind his own business, saying that the Muslims at Bhagalpur had murdered young children.

Nate Khan was visibly Muslim and he naturally took fright, but luckily, there was a security picket at the ghat where Shakaldev Singh made him take shelter, and having deposited him in (supposedly) safe hands he crossed over.

We don't know whether Nate Khan is alive or chopped to pieces! Communal riots are spreading to the rural areas and that's a bad sign.

Incidentally, Pakistan won a tumultuous victory

over India at the Eden Grounds, Calcutta, and I won't be surprised if riots begin in Calcutta. Muslims will obviously celebrate. There's enough fire already and just a little Muslim mirth will be spark enough to light it into an inferno. I'll keep my fingers crossed!

28 October 1989

Curfew relaxed, more bodies were found and a warder saw a truckload of them being taken to the river. They were all decomposed and piled higgledy-piggledy and bouncing like sponge as the truck moved over the rough road full of potholes. Escorted by a jeepload of policemen, they had muffled their mouths to avoid the stink of decayed bodies. I asked whether the bodies were of Muslims or Hindus, and the warder replied 'Who knows for the violence has been "secular" and both Hindus and Muslims have been killed indiscriminately.' All he knew was that the dead stink, whether they be Hindus or Muslims!

The radio later announced that eighteen dead bodies had been found, which was obviously untrue.

As dusk fell, and I was locked in for the night, I heard powerful bomb blasts.

The Mandals, Bhinds, and Ghoris live along the Ganges or the islands in the river and they live by crime. It's difficult for the forces of law to reach them, as the riverine tracts, their dwellings, are full of marshes, bogs, and undergrowth. They are all Hindus. They rob and kill weary and unsuspecting travellers, and show no mercy—they chop their victims into little pieces and throw them into the river after looting them.

On the 26 October, a warder was on a ferry when he saw four Muslims board another ferry in midstream. The Muslims he says were ambushed by the Mandal tribe and killed.

It's unsafe for Muslims to venture out, especially in the strongholds of the Mandals, Bhinds, and Ghoris. These people steal into Bhagalpur town in the dead of night and resort to looting and burning. They are desperate and when resisted by the police, they retreat to their strongholds in the marshes of the river.

But I have had the Mandals and the Bhinds work for me here and they have been good to me and served me well. They are quarrelsome and don't like others treading in their domain. Woe betide the person who intrudes upon them! Like camels they nurse their grouse!

29 October 1989

Devi Tiwari, the warder, informed me this morning that it was Jha, the DM, who personally tried to lead the Ram Shila puja[16] through the Muslim-dominated area near

[16] Consecration of bricks to lay the foundation of the Ram Janamsthan temple in Ayodhya.

the mosque. Muslim women climbed to the rooftops and began beating their breasts and shouting in chorus, 'Hai re hindhua!'

This infuriated their men and they began attacking the mob with great vigour. These gory tales are so painful but I must record them and keep myself busy or else I may break down myself.

Baij Nath Thakur, the clerk, was here too this morning and said that it was discipline and a government job that was restraining him. Passions are running high, and few people have stopped to think rationally. For most, madness has overtaken their thinking and cruelty their hearts! Thakur says that some people have started calling me a 'devta' because had I not been here and such a well-guarded prisoner, the CRPF wouldn't have been posted here either and had that been the case, thousands and thousands more would have perished! At least my incarceration has been of some use, if that's the case!

My rations are beginning to run out. I have just a little rice left and the cornflakes Geeta brought me. I practically live on these.

Today is Diwali and I have given the cook, bearer, and gardener a tin of condensed milk to make themselves something sweet. It's all I could offer them.

It's another sad Diwali for me. I still haven't got over the shock of the destruction of the Golden Temple and the killings of 1984 and here I am witnessing a fresh bout of bloodletting, mayhem, and destruction.

Victuals in the prison godown are running low and since all the contractors are Muslim and are in hiding, poor souls, there's no one to restock the godown. If the supplies finish, there's no telling what may happen, and the prisoners may riot.

There are searches going on in the town and the authorities have recovered gunpowder, bombs, and ammunition in great quantities. On 5 November it will be Guy Fawkes Day. What was it?: 'Remember, remember, the fifth of November, the Gunpowder Treason and plot', or something to this effect.

The radio announced this morning at 8 a.m. that curfew would be lifted and I was somewhat surprised because I was hearing bomb blasts while listening to the news and last night hadn't been quiet either. Head warder Karoo Singh, a good Rajput, has just come in at 12 p.m. and tells me that military vehicles were seen around town announcing that curfew wouldn't be lifted and anyone defying it would be shot on sight. I have reports that the situation has deteriorated since yesterday's relaxation of the curfew and a CRPF officer has been shot dead. I am recording whatever I hear and whatever source I can tap.[17] I am beginning to run out of ballpoints. I rummaged through all my belongings and luckily, found this one.

[17] Here the writing is faint.

It doesn't have a fine point and is brittle. Never mind. Beggars can't be choosers.

Neetia Mandal, I have observed, has been putting in extra effort to serve me and has become more pleasant. He never leaves the barrack and isn't as restless as he was before. Maybe he's heard the 'devta' story!

But later I learn from a warder that that's not the case, and Neetia is more devoted because he's had a dream that he was my son in his last life and hadn't looked after me as a son should so he's redoubling his efforts to make me as comfortable as he possibly can under the circumstances. I don't mind at all. Being pampered by anyone here is a luxury and I'm enjoying the devotion!

30 October 1989

The socialists in Spain have retained their majority in the Cortez in a general election held yesterday. The extremists have made gains and so have the conservatives at the cost of the centrists.

Mishra, the senior warder, informs me that the Bharatiya Janata Party is helping the Hindus in the lootings and killings. J.L. Arya is the home secretary here in Bihar. The doctor came at 9.40 a.m. and said that the Supreme Court had given directions to the chief election commissioner to have my nomination papers filed. It means that the government was obstructing the process. The doctor also told me that 500 people had been arrested and were now in our jail. They were in poor health, with wounds, bruises, and broken limbs. He put the toll of dead at 1,000. He also said that the riots were spreading to the rural areas. A warder informed me that yesterday's curfew was very tight and two Hindus riding a motorcycle in Tika Mandi were shot dead with a machine-gun burst.

At 2.30 p.m. Shukla Baboo came and told me that my local counsel, Mr Mishra, had come for the 'allegiance to the Constitution' oath.[18] So I accompanied him to the superintendent's office, where in the presence of the jailor, Satish Baboo, Mr Mishra administered the oath in Hindi which I duly signed and he attested. All the formalities were completed by 2.52 p.m., well before the deadline for filing for nomination—3 p.m., 30 October 1989.

Mr Mishra was pale as death. I asked him what was wrong, was he sick? No he replied, it was fear that had given him this ashen look. He said that the Muslims in town were slaughtering the Hindus and that the curfew was very tight–the army had taken over completely.

I asked the jailor to have Mr Mishra sent home with a police escort or patrol and he said he would. Satish Baboo

[18] Papa had to swear his allegiance to the Constitution of India before he could file his nomination for the 1989 Lok Sabha elections. By this time, he was president of the Akali Dal. The Sikhs at the time felt that he was the solution to the Punjab problem.

escorted me back to my enclosure. On the walk back, I thought of my counsel's mutterings about the Muslims slaughtering the Hindus.

Sardar Nirmal Singh (Bhaiji) who looks after our welfare here says he'd gone to a Muslim lawyer to engage him for our case but he succumbed to Congress pressure and declined the brief. Whatever I may have said about the Muslims here, there's still no reason why they shouldn't receive the protection of the law and why they shouldn't be treated as fellow human beings.

Rioting, arson, and killings have spread to Banka, Amarpur, and a homestead belonging to Muslims, Mirzapur, across the river. Thana Beypore has been razed to the ground and all its inhabitants killed. They won't be able to control the devastation and fury in the rural areas mainly because the administration will look the other way and then it takes time for information to reach, which acts as a good enough alibi for its connivance and inaction. K.C. Pant, the defence minister, is about to quit.

There is further news of Nate Khan, very sad I'm afraid. I have been informed that some youths attacked him on the railway line and finished him off. His body has been disposed of at Thana Beypore, a place famous for xylography, across the river. The craftsmen do beautiful carvings on wood there.

I heard a lot of blasts but they may have been Diwali crackers. Last night I didn't have my barrack lit with diyas in deference to the people killed. Nate Khan's murder has disturbed me deeply.

Earlier today, at 8.45 a.m., Ganguli was sent by the jailor to ask me what district the constituency Tarn Taran lay in. I wrote out a chit saying 'Amritsar'.

31 October 1989

I have had a new bed made of rotten-leaf compost for my flowers and put in more seeds, just in case the first lot in earthen pots fails. The curfew has been lifted for two hours only but I hear the people are in a state of shock for nothing of this kind has ever happened in Bhagalpur before, and so they are scared. In any case, they'll be able to stretch their legs and buy their victuals.

The doctor came and cheered me up and said that no Congressman will have the courage to stand against me in the elections. I needed a good word, for today I'm in the dumps. I don't know why.

No green veggies at all. I ate a roti with some chollian di daal and there was some curd, over which I sprinkled some sugar. I liked curd and enjoyed the crunch-crunch of the sugar between my molars.

Any government which is formed after a great struggle must have a very clear political, economic, and social goal. A government formed on retribution and revenge cannot last. An ideology is a must.

After World War II, the reconstruction of Europe would have failed had the Marshall Plan not been in place and the governments formed had based their programmes on revenge and the Nuremberg trials alone. Look what's happened in Argentina recently. The government formed after the Falklands War collapsed because of retribution and only imprisoned the guilty during the Dirty War and the debacle of the Falklands War. This government had no political, economic, or social goals. What about Robespierre? And now the Gandhi government.

I'm convinced that without an ideology a government, no matter how noble, will collapse if its very motive is revenge. On the other hand if retribution can be curbed and is tempered with political ideology that government will endure. So there can be Nuremberg plus the Marshall Plan but not the former without the latter.

George Marshall was the US Secretary of State (1947 to 1949) and he initiated the European Recovery Programme. In 1953 he was awarded the Nobel Prize for Peace.

I did have a feeling that Pant would ditch Gandhi, as he is a bit too honorable to tell so many lies. I wasn't very surprised to hear him accuse Mr Gandhi of deception and monopolizing power in a coterie of inexperienced bureaucrats and corrupt politicians.

My gardener, Geeta Ram Yadav, a dacoit, is a very versatile man. He was carrying a sackful of farmyard manure from near the bogs earlier today; when he brought it to the verandah and unloaded it he found two scorpions. He captured them both. I heard a commotion and found all the three warders and the duty clerk bending over him. There was much excitement.

I went to enquire. I was surprised to see him holding a scorpion and demonstrating how the sting is taken out of the tail. There was vicarious pleasure, with the little audience clapping and laughing with juvenile mirth. I didn't enjoy the spectacle for there was cruelty in what the gardener did, but I suppose the option was to kill the scorpions.

After I was locked in, I heard some booms and rifle fire. There is trouble and it hasn't abated. The poor are in a deplorable state. Some of the daily-wage earners from the Bengali refugee colony came begging for food, risking the tight curfew, into the jail family quarters, and everyone who could afford to was generous in giving.

I said a lot of prayers and meditated and so by the evening I was fit as a fiddle. The morning's gloom had disappeared, I ate well at supper and went to sleep calm.

1 November 1989

It's a fine morning, helicopters are hovering above the jail and the officers must be scouting the area. The army hasn't been able to snuff out the trouble and it continues to confuse and befuddle the government. The DM and the police had the intelligence and they knew that the Muslims would resist and confront any Hindu procession, so I don't know why they allowed the Shila puja procession to go through well-fortified Muslim strongholds. If they had to allow it, they could have at least arrested the desperate troublemakers from amongst the Hindus and Muslims, disarmed the latter, and made a strong show of force by making heavy deployments, along the route as well as on the rooftops, bringing in the mounted police and tear gas squads. To allow the Hindu procession without these precautions was either madness or complete professional amateurishness. The whole of Bihar is up in flames, as a result of the DM's and SP's folly.

The doctor came and said he'd seen today's papers and he says I'll be contesting against one Ajit Singh from Tarn Taran.

Dachau, Bhagalpur

Martin Luther was a German Augustinian monk who visited Rome in 1510–11 and was appalled by the wealth, corruption, and profligacy of the papacy. His work led to his writing out a charter which in 1517 he nailed to the chapel door at Wattenberg Castle. In this he attacked the papal indulgences. In 1520 he launched the Protestant Reformation, publicly burning a papal bill of condemnation against himself. For doing this he was excommunicated in 1521. He refused to recant and was sheltered by the Elector of Saxony.

That's all that Luther did and I have done no more than that! I wrote to the government of the crimes it was committing against the Sikh people, and the government, corrupt and profligate like the papal church, took umbrage and has confined me to severe solitary confinement since my capture in 1984.

I have committed no crime by listing out the tortures, indignities, and the denial of constitutional and human rights to the Sikhs. Somebody like Luther had to be repelled by the above and object. It's just a coincidence that I have filled the slot and stuck it out without compromising or denying what I have written. It's the writings, not the killings, that disturb tyrants and the corrupt.

Some journalists have called me a rebel. Had I rebelled, I would have said so in no uncertain terms. The fact is I haven't done anything of the sort. When a regime uses brutal force over an unarmed people, it loses its moral right to rule and the people who submit to such a rule commit a grave injustice against themselves.

British rule in India did not end in 1947—it ended in

1918, when the British used brutal force at Jallianwala Bagh. In 1947, the British merely handed over power formally. The illegitimate and immoral force used by Delhi against the Sikhs in 1984 and since then has placed the New Delhi police in a similar dilemma.

Mark Tully, in the BBC broadcast at 8.30 p.m. this evening, announced that Satish Jacob in Bhagalpur had informed him that the army had handed over a 100 Muslims of Chandali village to the police, of whom thirty-eight had been killed. The whereabouts of the remaining, save four, were not known and an inquiry had been ordered. He further disclosed that twenty bodies of students had been found in a well on the university campus. The information trickling in to me has some basis as is proved by this account.

The curfew was lifted after a long spell and I received one Delhi paper, the *Hindustan Times.* According to the press, I am going to be one of the main candidates in the parliamentary poll.

The jail authorities sent me a cauliflower and three tomatoes and I ate a hearty supper after many days without fresh green vegetables. It's only when such bounties are not given that one appreciates their value. I have rarely missed green veggies before, save in Tihar Jail, where they were not supplied and I was given rotten, stale ones.

2 November

Curfew is easing. There is more movement. Military aircraft are busy surveying the trouble spots. Satish Jacob of the BBC is still in town. He announced on BBC that the official death count is placed at 295. Eight hundred people are missing and presumed dead. Satish Jacob's army informant told him that many dead bodies were floating down the Ganges. The centre of town has been destroyed by looting and arson. The informant said the situation was steadier and the town was limping towards normalcy and sanity.

I have had the chrysanthemums tied to thin sticks, as their stalks were not strong enough to stay erect. My left knee pains and it's getting worse. When I sit cross-legged to pray I can barely sit for an hour, for my knee aches. In the evening, reciting the Rehraas Sahib, I put my arm around my knee like a crutch and that gives some relief.[19]

Loyalty is a sentiment. It's an emotion, not a physical commodity which can be sold or bartered. It has to be won, not purchased. It cannot be won by repression or torture because these have a physical content. It is won through love, through the exercise of higher words and spiritual power. Therefore, no amount of physical torture, a life behind bars or camel loads of rubies, pearls, and

[19] Papa's knees were severely injured during torture.

sapphires can make me loyal to a system which does not respect my shrines, the lives of my people, the honour of my mothers, sisters, and daughters and all that I consider worthy of respect.

3 November 1989

Pathak, the senior warder, is here. He informs me that the CRPF men turned a blind eye to the Hindus who set the shops and homes of Muslims ablaze with petrol provided free by a Marwari. He says that the Muslims have been bashed badly. Communal hatred reigns supreme and it's dreadful to hear such cruel and inhumane things.

Sikandar is a young man who lights the lamps, morning, evenings, and night. He looks like a chimney sweep, for his clothes are full of oil and dark with grime. He keeps everyone in good humour, with his jokes and dances.

One day during the monsoon when it was pouring and the warders were in the corridor, he danced around the bearded Nate Khan. Nate Khan, who was short of humour, took umbrage and gave poor Sikandar a tight slap which sent him spinning—he remained in a daze for days.

Today Sikandar came to light the lamps while I was having my evening walk. I asked him to pray for Nate Khan's soul. Sikandar told me ill-humouredly that even if Nate hadn't slapped him he wouldn't pray for him as he wished all Muslims dead with no exceptions! The hatred is very deep.

A warder has come from Patna and he says that at the Hanuman temple near the railway station the slogan 'Jaise jaise Hindu jaga hai, teseh, teseh Muslim bhagah hai' is heard. The temple is in the midst of a Muslim population and he fears trouble at any moment.

The market has opened and there's much hustle and bustle. The godown people sent me all the essentials—eggs, fruit, veggies, tea, dal. I received the papers. It's such a joy to see things coming in normally. I heard no bangs and I, therefore, suppose the Hindus and Muslims have called it a day. They have inflicted such immeasurable harm on each other. If I hadn't been imprisoned in this Hindu heartland I would never have known their minds—here I have had a ringside view.

A warder tells me that as one alights from the train at the station one gets a sight of the devastation. He says that the gutters stink to high heavens and the smell of death hangs all around. I think that they haven't been able to remove the dead bodies. It's so sad and pathetic and many of the dead are being washed down the Ganga, that is the ones who are fortunate. In death, too, one needs fortune and luck!

The BBC says that Gandhi's Congress is in disarray and totally demoralized and hasn't been able to bring out a manifesto yet.

I ate a good, hearty supper. There were eggs, cauliflower, potatoes, and Cadbury chocolate for pudding.

It's chilly now and the evening cold water bath doesn't agree with me, though I love it very much for it rejuvenates me and takes away the fatigue of the day. I shall continue the cold water bath for as long as I can bear it. Once it gets too cold, I shall add the luxury of a few mugs of hot water, but bathe I must.

4 November 1989

Last night, apart from draping myself with a bedsheet, I had to cover myself with a woollen shawl. Winter is finally here, and what joy, I had a normal breakfast. Apples after days!

We caught a bandicoot after a long spell. Mukhia, the bearer, said it was a giant and that it smelt foul. He threw it in the gutter which carries the refuse out. Every time a bandicoot is trapped and disposed of in this manner, I feel so happy and say to myself that at least it's going out of jail and into liberty and freedom.

Netia, the cook, and Sita Ram, the gardener, are busy making the vijayanti seed rosaries as I'll be having visitors soon. They have three needle-like iron rods, brought red hot out of the coal fire and then they quickly prick the seed. It's a cumbersome job because the seed doesn't get pricked in one go, and the needles have to go back in the fire two or three times, which destroys some seeds. A lot of toil goes into making a rosary.

A warder who came from town informed me that the police has disposed of the seriously wounded along with the dead. This is what the army did in Amritsar in 1984 during Operation Blue Star as well. It is said here that had they not taken these steps, the casualty figures would have risen very high and the government wants to keep them to the lowest.

Many ask me that aren't we all Hindus and I merely smile saying nothing. I can't forget that I'm their prisoner and the havoc wrought by them on our religion, our polity, and our society.

My silence and aloofness is my revenge. I keep quiet and accept any favours with a smile without causing affront or letting them know what I think.

My heart bleeds for the dead amongst the Hindus and Muslims and for those rendered homeless. There is extreme poverty here and the riots have aggravated the already hopeless conditions of the poor.

In the evening, after I had said my prayers and was preparing for my daily walk, the special commissioner accompanied by the assistant commissioner and jail superintendent came to see me and ask me if I had any grievances. I told him about my teeth, urinary problem, and the knee, and about my books—simple ones like *Just William* and *Best Crime Stories* were confiscated and labelled objectionable 'apatijanak'—and the crude manner in which my family was made to meet me.

The special commissioner noted everything and said he'd take necessary action and said I could call him whenever I needed, for which I thanked him.

In the evening, after I was locked in, there was a terrible riot in Tika Mandi and I heard women and children shrieking. I learnt later that a truckload of Muslim toughs had come to set the Hindu homes ablaze but they were captured and their plans thwarted.

Had cauliflower cutlets with HP sauce and fresh orange juice for supper. A real treat!

5 November1989

It was a chilly night, I see the warders in their sweaters and shawls. There was no fruit for breakfast so I ate cornflakes (gift from GI).

My toffees are about to finish and Too-too loves one every morning. I hope someone comes from home but perhaps they'll be too busy with the elections. The BBC announced this morning that the majority of those killed here in the riots were Muslims. The jail, too, is full of them, some 500, along with a few Hindus.

The communists in Punjab have got together and are very cross with the Akali Dal for supporting me. They profess to represent the working and toiling classes here but go for their own medical treatment to Russia. Mr Harkrishan Singh Surjit has just been there and holidayed at Sevastopol on the Black Sea. I haven't heard of greater frauds. In Punjab they have behaved like fifth columnists and informers of the Congress and had our youth captured or killed by the heartless forces of the Centre. The Akali Dal will have to begin a programme of reconstruction in the rural areas and city centres. Good schooling for the underprivileged, good technical training for them, and jobs.

It's been a little warm today, none of my winter seeds have popped. I have been sent fruit, eggs, and veggies too. Today, Sunday, I listened to two of my favourite programmes on the BBC. 'Anything Goes' by Bob H[20] is a great show and you can ask the host to play anything, a song, a tune, a speech, or even tigers roaring. The other is 'A Letter from America' by Alistair Cooke.

Cooke wasn't his usual self this evening but I admire his diction and his spontaneity. At 10.45 p.m. there was a tremendous bang. The loudest burst I have heard yet. A warder told me that the sound came from Berari—that's one area that's remained unaffected by this insanity so far. Things won't deteriorate to what they were when all the madness first began because the forces are more vigilant

[20] Robert Holness presented the BBC World Service Show 'Anything Goes', a show said to be a favourite of Aung San Suu Kyi when she was house arrest, bringing him a legion of international fans.

and determined to avoid trouble. However, it bodes ill, for this was a peaceful suburb and the Hindus and Muslims are divided equally.

Mukhia, my bearer, enlightened me much this morning about friendship. I asked him whether he had any friends here and he said that he was done with them forever for they were the source of all his troubles and his present plight.[21] Later I heard Eartha Kitt, the famous singer, in a BBC interview repeat the same sentiment. She said friends become jealous, let one down, and cause grave unhappiness. It all boils down to what Voltaire said long ago, 'God save me from my friends, I can take care of my enemies myself.'

6 November 1989

It was chilly last night, and I thought I'd need a blanket. I'll have the blanket taken out of the mothballs and aired.

The chrysanthemums have come to bud but their stalks are full of those tiny black insects that hang on like claws and won't go away. I have asked for the senior warder who has done a course in plant protection and the jailor said he'd send him. I hope he does. The gladioli have also come into bud and I may soon have a bloom of these most gorgeous flowers. But they won't bloom before

[21] All the people deputed to work for Papa were prisoners in the same jail.

8 November and I was so looking forward to their doing so, for Bibiji and GI may be here and I wanted to greet them with gladioli. Neetia Mandal, my cook, has completed the rosaries of the vijayanti seeds and I have one each for the children. He says I won't be here much longer as he had dreamt that I had a fabulous lead over my rival—for every vote cast in his favour seven were cast for me. He says the ratio will be seven to one.[22]

The most famous pianist of this century, Vladimir Horowitz, a Russsian émigré, died in New York today. He specialized in Chopin. His critics found him too loud but most music lovers will remember him forever. He always believed that the mind, the heart, and the finger must coordinate so as to strike the right note. He endeavoured to do just that and won an immortal place in musical history. Good luck and farewell!

The migraine has not gone. I will eat a hearty meal—daal rice sabzi and papad and swallow a pill, Proxyvon[23]—and then lie down in the hope that I get up for my evening walk well and out of pain. I will, however, miss out on the Sukhmani Sahib, which I try not to as it gives me great peace and solace.

A lovely soft cool breeze blows through my windows and the birds are chirping, though the harmony is broken by the loud angry notes of the mynahs. The squirrels are

[22] In reality, the lead was about 4.5 lakh, the largest ever then in India.

[23] For the headache.

pottering around trying to burrow a passage through the paddy straw I have thrown over the seedlings and eat whatever has sprouted. They are very destructive creatures though they look innocent and harmless.

The pain hasn't abated. I got up and sat out in the garden under the jamun tree. Looking at the green made me feel slightly better but the discomfort continued. I gulped down glasses full of hot black coffee but there was only a marginal change. I bathed with cold water, which was soothing. Then they locked me in for the night.

The insects that hover about the light have become fewer. I could read for somewhat longer. I received the *Hindustan Times*, *TOI*, and the *Indian Express*. The BBC has begun the reading of *Tess of the D'ubervilles* by Thomas Hardy in twenty serials. Hardy writes sad stories.

7 November 1989

Rumours abound. Even the BBC has not been able to project the truth. Lots and lots of people have died and what I have been noting is quite close to the truth. This morning I was amazed at what a warder asked me. He wanted to know whether the local AIG, a Muslim, had been arrested. I said I didn't know as I hadn't heard it over the radio or read it in the papers. He looked surprised and said he had heard from the horse's mouth that the Muslim police officer had been passing secret messages to Pakistan on a clandestine wireless set. I told him this couldn't be true and assured him that no officer of the rank of an AIG would be naïve enough to pass messages on the wireless as he would be detected in no time.

A senior warder came and had my chrysanthemums sprayed with insecticide and gave me some urea for them. He also gave me some carrot seeds. Sweet of him.

The riots have spread to Sasaram where the mausoleum of Sher Shah Suri lies. Curfew has been imposed and the army is out. There's been looting and burning and several people have died.

Someone must have arrived from home as tomorrow I'm to be produced in court. But the jailor says it's highly unlikely as the situation was tense and curfew may be reimposed.

It's the Ram Shila puja and bricks are going to Ayodhya and on 9 November the Hindus will lay the foundation stone of Lord Rama's temple and demolish the mosque at the site.

In the evening I didn't walk as I had a migraine but this time I was determined not to eat a painkiller. Therefore, before being locked in I had a cold bath and immediately after, inhaled steam full of Vicks. Strangely, the migraine disappeared and I sat down to read the papers and eat an omelette and chips for dinner.

It's swiftly coming on to winter and it's chilly. I slept under a blanket and in the early hours of the morning, I wished I'd kept my shawl besides me for I may have used it. I was too lazy to get up and fetch it from the chair.

The insects are disappearing and there are fewer lizards—the horrible creatures have gone to hibernate for the winter.

8 November 1989

The trouble in Sasaram continues. The Hindus have claimed that the mausoleum of Sher Shah Suri is a Shiva temple.

In America they are going to have a black mayor for New York and a black governor in Virginia. Both are unprecedented events, especially the latter, as Virginia is a south conservative state and went to war on the question of slavery. The world is changing but here the bigotry continues.

I was to appear in court today but they didn't send me. I heard Geeta and Teddy Bhayaji had come and I was thrilled. In the evening Pandey, the assistant jailor, came and said I had an interview. I accompanied him to the gate and asked him what he'd done to the warders who'd created a din from 3 to 6 a.m., not letting me sleep. He said he'd given them a piece of his mind and reported the matter to the jailor.

I was bitterly disappointed when I met Mr Mishra, my lawyer, through the bars. He said Geeta hadn't come but

Teddy Sahib had, whom I could see, sitting far away. His verification papers had not been cleared by the police. Just imagine, he's been coming here for the last four years and even the cats know who he is but the authorities don't!

Bibiji sent me the yellow shawl which she'd sent me in the winter of 1985–86 and has been sending ever since. It's come again for the fourth winter and let's hope it's the last year at this Dachau.[24] Geeta sent me my woollen nightsuits and tuck and I was given some vegetables.

Mr Mishra said the next court date was fixed for 7 December. Good God, I said, they are really detaining us. It was dusk when they shut me in. I was pleasantly surprised to hear that Nate Khan, the senior Muslim warder who was believed killed in the riots, was alive and safe. I thanked God for he did pray to Allah for me.

9 November 1989

The BBC announced that amidst mounting tension, the Hindus have captured the disputed land near the Babri Masjid. Mishra, the warder, and Thakur, the clerk, were here this morning and they all talked of violence. Mishra said that once the colleges opened, the students would go on a rampage.

I had a trying day. God bless Mr Anant Ram and Mr

[24] Papa would send all his woollens back home, for he had no place to store them.

Berari who had me tortured so brutally by placing an iron roller between my knees and forcing a policeman down to sit on them while bending them to press my knees to my back. I can now barely sit on my haunches, Indian, fashion, even to take a dump! (Because my WC is out of commission I had to use the lavatory outside and my God, how my knees pained and continued paining for hours afterwards.) I think my tendons must be torn or something.

The *TOI* reports with great bias against me that the militants are supporting me and that I may just lose because the Congress will get the Hindu and the Dalit vote.

Some of the glads are about to pop. In the eastern court, Sitaram has finished weeding the glads and chrysies. In the evening, the jailor sent me a garden chair and some raisins and Wilson[25] refills brought by Sardar Nirmal Singh or Baiji[26] as he was called.

The garden chair reclines as you push it back. Curfew at night continues and daily provisions are very dear. Sugar is selling at Rs 13 a kg. China's strongman, Deng,[27] has resigned. They say he's making way for a peaceful transfer of power after his death.

---

[25] Wilson pens.

[26] Charan Singh's friend and associate who was a great help during the prison years.

[27] Deng Xiaoping, who resigned from his post of Chairman of the Chinese Central Military Commission in 1989

10 November 1989

I heard the call of a partridge early this morning. It was chilly despite the blanket and the shawl.

Another icon in the communist world has fallen, the chief of the Bulgarian Communist Party. It's a historic epoch. The Berlin Wall has also been breached, built twenty-eight years ago to keep in the East Germans. Today it was opened and thousands of East Germans poured into a free world. It's a historic moment and before long it will lead to the unification of the German people.

The Hindus are flushed with success with the foundation-laying ceremony at Ayodhya. The jailor told me belligerently when he came to see me in the evening that the Muslims could go away if they didn't like it. In the evening they lit earthen lamps and burst crackers till late into the night only to add further to Muslim alienation. I tuned into Pakistan radio to hear the Muslim reaction and sure enough, Benazir Bhutto had stepped into the Hindu–Muslim quarrel. She called it the wilful desecration of a Muslim holy place and called upon the Indian government to stop discrimination against the Muslims.

My WC has been finally settled, much to my relief. I take my hurricane lamp and radio to my little partitioned lavatory and plonk myself down on to the pot and listen to the BBC.

11 November 1989

A warder told me this morning that though they had celebrated the laying of the foundation at Ayodhya, their joy would not be complete till the Babri Masjid was knocked down. This growing bigotry must be fought.

If they didn't spare the Golden Temple, everything else is chicken feed for these fanatics! At 12.15 p.m., a warder who had just entered the gate told me that all rickshaw-pullers, pedestrians, and people in tempos were fleeing for their lives and safety as they had heard that the Muslims in Tarkarpur had begun killing Hindus. It was a frightening rumour.

I sat out most of the day under the jamun in my new garden chair. I asked the jailor if I could get some seedlings from the Agricultural University but he said the town was still disturbed and so he couldn't do so. Perhaps I may not have a pretty garden this winter for most of my seeds have failed to germinate.

I had samosas for lunch with chutney and tomato sauce. They were wonderful. I like eating them formally with a fork and knife—you see, if I eat them with my hands I think I'm having a snack and psychologically I feel I haven't eaten a full meal.

The Indian government has condemned Benazir Bhutto's statement and charged her with malicious meddling.

12 November 1989

I didn't sleep very well last night. I think the Congress is going to meet its Waterloo and a wave is fast building which will wash it away.

Spotted doves, symbolic of peace, in my flowerbeds this morning, pecking gently and quietly for their food.

Yesterday's news has been confirmed by the BBC, saying that 200 houses have been burnt near here. A warder told me that all the houses belonged to Hindus and some 500 of them had been killed. It may be an exaggeration, but I'm writing it down nevertheless as later, such reports are normally confirmed.

The Hindus are quite scared even though they are in an overwhelming majority. The local Muslims are exhorting their men to sell their gold and buy arms, I don't know where all this will lead. The BJP is becoming more strident and they say it has long-term goals, that is, to not capture power now but to work up the Hindus to a pitch so that by the next election it becomes a predominant power in Parliament and attains its avowed goal of making this country into a Hindu rashtra. I am horrified. Without such a rashtra our holy shrines have been knocked down, our womenfolk raped, our youth eliminated, judicial murders, illegal detentions carried out without a trial. I wonder what they'll do once a rashtra is declared.

In Sindh province, in a tit-for-tat bid, the Muslims have attempted to set Hindu temples ablaze. The forces have intervened and made some arrests but Pakistan has hardly any Hindu population to attack, and to attack their places of worship is as ridiculous as Don Quixote battling the windmills. In any case such wanton acts indicate a very low IQ and poor upbringing.

13 November 1989

Today was Guru Nanak's birthday. We had a langar. Netia Mandal, Mukhia, Sitaram, Too-too, and I constituted the sangat. We ate puris, allu gobi, and kheer. I opened a tin of condensed milk and there was half a kilo of milk and raisins—all together they made a very good kheer. Sitaram ate thirty-five puris and he didn't miss his jail meal either! In fact they all ate their jail meal and what they ate at the langar was extra. Extraordinary eaters!

In the evening we lit the barrack with candles and some earthen lamps. Neetia put a lamp at the base of each tree and each flower pot. He felt this was auspicious.

My heart missed a beat because the glads are coming into flower—fortunately, they didn't come to any harm. The lit up ward looked beautiful and reminded me of the aarti we recite before going to sleep.

I began reading the biography of Benazir Bhutto. I was almost in tears when she described her father's last day and her last visit. I could share her thoughts as I have been in the death cell myself.

14 November 1989

Mr Mishra took my signature on a form to appoint election agents and my power of attorney. He said he was going to see the others[28] in the camp jail. While I was sitting with the jailor, a host of Muslim prisoners, leaders of Bhagalpur, amongst them a lawyer and a maulvi, came and sat with me and put forward their grouses before the jailor. They were extremely dirty and their faces looked harsh. I felt uncomfortable in their presence, didn't utter a word, and then the jailor asked Lanan, the clerk, to escort me to my barrack. Mr Mishra said that there's a lot of fear—it's the twenty-third day of curfew and it's still continuing. He said that he's afraid to venture out himself. He said he'd move a bail application for the others in the special judges' court. The High Court has fixed 14 December for a decision.

I hear the Cole Porter show once a week on BBC and it's very interesting. I'll ask Geeta to collect all his songs and lyrics.

[28] Papa's co-accuseds, who were together in another jail. Papa was in solitary confinement. Mishra was their lawyer.

15 November 1989

The jailor came in the evening and said they would allow my lawyer to have me photographed[29] but not from behind bars, he added. And I said, why on earth should I have myself photographed from behind bars? However, everything went off well. I look forward to meeting Mr Mishra tomorrow, on any pretext whatsoever. For it's lovely to meet anyone from outside.

16 November 1989

In the evening, the senior warder brought me some dahlias, Californian poppies, and some other plants whose names he didn't know but they look like lupins. The bazaar is shut today too as the RSS leaders' protest has provoked anguish amongst the Hindus. Mr Mishra, my lawyer, came along with the photographer. I was taken towards the factory end and under the pipal tree, the photographer clicked me in three different poses. The photographer said he'd give Mr Mishra the negative, give me three photographs and the jail authorities three. The jailor was deadly scared to have the jail wall form the background. Yesterday he said the bars wouldn't be allowed. I don't know why they're in such panic.

---

[29] He had to be photographed so he could file his nomination.

There are no papers today, none at all. Shukal Babu said I'd get no tea and I must make do with coffee. I like my coffee but I can't do without my tea mornings and evenings. Since the bazaar is shut I have to drink coffee till the tea comes.

17 November 1989

The photographs haven't been delivered.

In El Salvador, the right-wing vigilante groups of the Arena[30] ruling party have shot down six intellectuals. These extrajudicial killings by the government can't be taken lightly, and must receive universal condemnation. If I were in Parliament, I'd say so categorically and have the government protest against such killings.

Two gladiolis are coming into bloom and they're a rich yellow. Extremely pretty. I love them so much but I fear their time will be over so soon. I should enjoy their present beauty and not think of the time of their withering away. The bazaar is going to be shut again I'm told, and there are going to be no provisions or papers.

I had a hairwash today and the barber came and cut my nails. He's a nice, quiet man. He told me that my former barber runs his own business and makes Rs 15 to 20 a day. He said the barbers outside charge Re 1 for cutting

[30] The Nationalist Republican Alliance (Allianza Republicana Nacionalista).

nails, Rs 2 for a shave, Rs 3 for a complete shave of the scalp, Rs 4 for a haircut, and Rs 2 for a head massage! I chat with him and elicit as much info of the outside world as I possibly can. It helps in keeping boredom away and keeps my mind active.

The jailor arrived with the photos they clicked yesterday. I have greyed a lot and my beard is a good salt and peppery one. There's a full-length photograph of mine under the pipal tree and the roots of the tree are visible. Which signifies that I have strong roots and my standing beneath it is also significant because nothing grows under the pipal and I have, with Waheguruji's grace, survived the toughest and most brutal form of imprisonment.

The curfew has been lifted completely, which includes the night curfew. I received my tea, papers and other provisions. I drank a glass of tea immediately and felt soothed.

18 November1989

I woke up to find dewdrops falling from the trees like rain—it was misty and nothing could be seen. I have seen such weather only once before in these last four years, in December 1985 when they brought me here. There was mist every morning and it wouldn't clear till almost noon and the langurs would huddle together on the roof of my cell for warmth. Today I haven't seen the langurs huddle in a group but all the other signs of a bitter winter are here. I hope it will be my last here.

A warder came beaming to me saying it's Janata all the way and the Congress is gone gone gone, clapping his hands in delight and said I'd be free soon.

The mist lifted after midday.

Had makki di roti and gobi allu for lunch. While I was cleaning a tooth, a toothpick broke in it. It meant trouble. I quickly sent a note to Dr Deo to call the dentist, who said he'd come tomorrow as in the afternoons and evenings he has a roaring private practice. I said I was in agony and must have the dentist forthwith. The poor man went and brought him—he extracted the broken bit of toothpick. He had to work hard and it pained me a lot. I bore the pain stoically as I had no option.

19 November 1989

It's misty again. The BBC and AIR say that the military has been put in charge of law and order. A warder told me that his contact in the police lines said that about three days ago, a senior army commander was here and the local brigadier told him nothing could be accomplished as the DM and the SP interfered too much. The matter has duly been reported to the home ministry—hence the order entrusting law and order to the army.

21 November 1989

I didn't note the events of 17 August 1989. I was taken to court as usual. Met Teddy Bhayaji, Bibiji, and Geeta. Teddy Bhayaji told me that the CJ of India had called my council, Sardar R.S. Sodhi, and said he wanted to solve the Punjab issue, and that something was in the offing. He said that the CJ[31] had told Sodhi that he'd visit the Golden Temple and bring Mr Gandhi and me face-to-face. I had been told to pack for Delhi and I did so, making an elaborate list of all that I was taking.

I was flown out at 3 p.m. in a BSF Beechcraft. From Palam, Delhi, I was driven to court within the Tihar Jail premises. I was made to wait for a long time in the prison van. It was hot and humid.

Eventually, they took me to court and Mr Khanna, the chief metropolitan magistrate, came in. He was kind and courteous and he said he'd let Dr Wadhera know I'd arrived. And that I would get all the facilities provided to me in Bhagalpur.

They then took me to my cell, the same one I was put in last time. Apart from the humiliating searches, I found that the height of the wall had been raised. On 18 August I spent the day within the cell's compound.

In the evening Dr Wadhera came to see me. I asked

[31] Chief Justice.

him to get me a radio, which he very sweetly did the next day after having an order passed by Mr Khanna.

That night at 11 p.m. I had a dreadful headache and asked for the doctor, who came on the 19th morning. Later I was marched to court. Mr Jethmalani was there along with the other lawyers. We got some time to talk. In the meantime, R.S. Sodhi made me sign a typed letter to the CJ of India which he had drafted with the approval of Mr Jethmalani and the CJ, saying that I believed in the Constitution, integrity etc. of India, and I would talk to the CJ on the Punjab situation. After I had signed it, it was attested by Mr Khanna.

Soon after I saw him rushing with great haste along with Dilloo Bhenji and R.S. Sodhi. Then they met the CJ who asked them to give a copy of what I'd signed to the press, to create the right atmosphere. That day, Mr Khanna committed the conspiracy case to the sessions court.

I was allowed to meet my family and eat the lunch they'd bought. I loved every moment of it. Inderjit Bhenji was there, Bibiji and Dads sat beside me, and Geeta served me my lunch.

After lunch, the justice told everyone to leave the court and I sat for a long time with my family. At about 3.30 p.m. I was taken back to jail.

On 20 August they flew me back to Bhagalpur.

22 November 1989

Balmy weather. I think polling will be heavy all over. Results won't start coming in till the 26th, that's Sunday.

A chap told me that Sardar Amrik S. Bhandari, a local Sikh, has gone to Tarn Taran to help out.[32] So sweet of him. His sons are safe[33] and the one who was injured in one of the bomb blasts is better though not completely well and his hearing is slightly impaired.

The second lot of seedlings have popped, and now I'll have all I want. I feel so satisfied.

23 November 1989

It's Geeta's birthday. She's in the midst of a battle up on platforms, canvassing support for me. I have sent her a telegram. Hope she receives it.

24 November 1989

Polling has been heavy all over. At night Sanjiv Gaur, a journalist speaking from Chandigarh for the BBC, said that the Simranjit S. Mann Akali Dal was the Akali party worth the name and that Badal, Tohra, Talwandi, and Barnala had been eclipsed.

---

[32] In the election campaign.

[33] The reference is to the local riots in Bhagalpur.

Bapuji electioneering for Pa in Taran Taran in 1989

25 November 1989

Only a day left for the poll in Punjab.

Dilloo Bhenji has very efficiently and single-handedly done tremendous work. She's arranged the alliances and let the party float and find its own level. She's a good strategist and I think she'll remain in charge of the party, its organization and its programmes.

They say I will triumph. It's in the hands of the Almighty—I pray and seek his blessings.

२५ पैसे

सत्यमेव जयते

भारत

TWENTYFIVE PAISE

प्रतिलिपि के लिए आवेदन की तारीख Date of application for the copy.	स्टाम्प और फोलिओ की अपेक्षित संख्या सूचित करने की निश्चित तारीख Date fixed for notifying the requisite number of stamps and folios.	अपेक्षित स्टाम्प और फोलिओ देने की तारीख Date of delivery of the requisite stamps and folios.	तारीख, जबकि देने के लिए प्रतिलिपि तैयार थी Date on which the copy was ready for delivery.	आवेदक को प्रतिलिपि देने की तारीख Date of making over the copy to the applicant.

In,

The Court of Special Judge,
Bhagalpur.

Spedial Case No.6/86.

State
Versus.
S.S.Mann and others ....Accused.

Order-sheet.

2.12.89 Sri Basudeo Prasad the Senior Special P.P.appeared and filed a petition praying to recallthe order of the date already fixed 7.12.89,as he would like to move a petition u/s 321 Cr.P.C.The defence counsels are also present.In the Special circumstances the prayer is allowed,Write to Supdts.central and Sp.Central Jail Bhagalpur to produce the accused persons in the court.

Heard Sri Basudeo Prasad Sp.P.P.incharge of the case as the petition to withdraw from the possession of the accused persons and put up for orders after examining the case record.

Sd/H.K.Verma
Special Judge.

lateron/2.12.89 ORDER.

This is order on the petition filed by Shri Basudeo Prasad,the Special Public Prosecutor and incharge of the case,soliciting consent to withdraw from the prosecution of the case under the provisions of section 321 of the Cr.P.C.

Moving the petition, Shri Basudeo Prasad, the Special Public Prosecutor, has submitted that the accused persons of the case are facing trial on various charges relating to offences in connection with disturbance in Punjab beginning from 1984.

In the recent General Election held in the country, accused Shri S.S.Mann and his five party colleagues have been elected to the Lok Sabha in a peaceful manner without any violence. So in view of changed situation, his attention has been drawn by the Government of Bihar that for the purpose of preserving peaceful atmosphere of good will and to bring about peaceful settlement of issues in the State of Punjab and the country it is in the Public interest to withdraw from the prosecution of the accused persons of the case. As he is convinced that it is in the larger interest of administration of justice so in the public interest consent should be accorded to withdraw from the prosecution of the case.

After hearing Shri Basudeo Prasad, the senior Public Prosecutor and incharge of the case and apprising with the reason which prompted him to withdraw from the

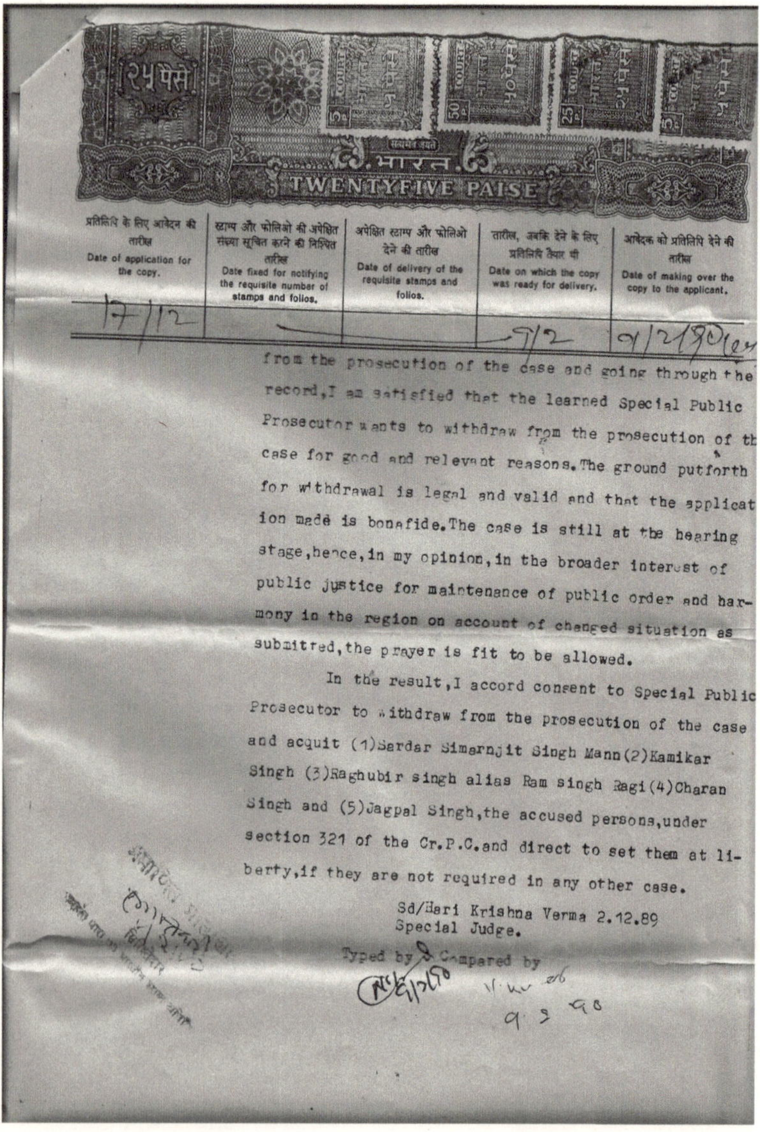

२५ पैसे

भारत

TWENTYFIVE PAISE

प्रतिलिपि के लिए आवेदन की तारीख Date of application for the copy.	स्टाम्प और फोलिओ की अपेक्षित संख्या सूचित करने की निश्चित तारीख Date fixed for notifying the requisite number of stamps and folios.	अपेक्षित स्टाम्प और फोलिओ देने की तारीख Date of delivery of the requisite stamps and folios.	तारीख, जबकि देने के लिए प्रतिलिपि तैयार थी Date on which the copy was ready for delivery.	आवेदक को प्रतिलिपि देने की तारीख Date of making over the copy to the applicant.
17/12	—		9/2	9/2/90

from the prosecution of the case and going through the record, I am satisfied that the learned Special Public Prosecutor wants to withdraw from the prosecution of the case for good and relevant reasons. The ground putforth for withdrawal is legal and valid and that the application made is bonafide. The case is still at the hearing stage, hence, in my opinion, in the broader interest of public justice for maintenance of public order and harmony in the region on account of changed situation as submitted, the prayer is fit to be allowed.

In the result, I accord consent to Special Public Prosecutor to withdraw from the prosecution of the case and acquit (1)Sardar Simarnjit Singh Mann (2)Kamikar Singh (3)Raghubir singh alias Ram singh Ragi (4)Charan Singh and (5)Jagpal Singh, the accused persons, under section 321 of the Cr.P.C. and direct to set them at liberty, if they are not required in any other case.

Sd/Hari Krishna Verma 2.12.89
Special Judge.

Typed by Compared by

9.2.90

26 November 1989

Polling started here early this morning. Here at the jail polling booth, Pelwan, the warder, said that all votes were going to the Janata Dal candidate. Wonder what's happening at home. The jailor, the doctor, and the chief head jamadar came and told me that polling in Punjab had been peaceful and that not a single booth had been captured nor an act of violence been committed.

The jailor said that voting had been between 60 and 65 per cent.

I was overjoyed. They all said I was on the pig's back. In the evening, the results and trends began to come in. They started with the south first where Mr Gandhi was expected to win and Karunanidhi, Ramarao, and Hegde collapsed like a pack of cards. In Gujarat, the tide against Gandhi began to turn. In MP and Rajasthan, the opposition held on fast, leaving UP, Bengal, and Bihar to gain the upper hand.

27 November 1989

I didn't sleep all night. I kept awake, listening to the results. In the south, the Congress has wiped out the DMK, TDP, and JD. In the north, from west to east, the Congress is being swept away.

My head aches badly. I lie down but there is no relief.

All day I could hardly stir as the pain was severe.

In the evening, Satish Babu came and said a TV report said I was doing well. Then Ram Iqbal Singh, the warder, came at 6 p.m. and said Dr Sahay had told him that I'd already taken a big lead of a lakh and 40,000 votes and that our candidates were making for the victory post.

I had a nice heavy supper, which brought considerable relief to my aching head. I went to bed early. I was very jittery the whole day and all night. Guru Arjan Sahib came to me in my thoughts and told me very clearly that I would win and that the panth would triumph, this was yesterday. But then I'm human and every time I have tried to rise, I have had to bite dust. Misfortune and hard conditions in jail have made me very pessimistic.

I kept my morale high with prayer and meditation. Late at night, a warder woke me up and told me I had taken a huge lead as had six of my other candidates. I thanked him and as soon as he left, I fell at the feet of Guru Nanak and prayed.

28 November 1989

I woke up this morning with my head clear and the migraine gone. At 6.20 a.m. I heard Satish Jacob, the BBC man, say that I was leading from Tarn Taran, with over four lakh votes and that the Congress was in for a rout in the Punjab.

Thakur, the clerk, came and told me to rise and give him some tea in celebration of the great event. At 11 a.m. AIR announced that I had won by four lakh and 80,000 votes. I felt sublime and humble. I thanked God. The news went on to say that all our candidates had won. It was a great occasion. Satish Baboo came and said Geeta had called but the line got disconnected.

I felt lovely. The jailor, Satish, and Ganguli Baboo came to congratulate me and I offered them a little piece of Amul chocolate, the only sweet I had, though I don't think Amul makes good chocolates.

In Bihar and UP, the Congress is suffering a great setback. It's a hung parliament. The commies are being a little humble but the BJP is gloating over its victory. I wonder how they'll be able to put together a coalition. Chandrashekhar and Devi Lal are running for the premier's office. I don't know how they'll deal with the Sikhs, but editorial comments in the Hindu national press are acerbic about our victory.

Yadav, the senior warder, sent me a bunch of healthy nasturtium plants. I had them put down in a bed beside the mango tree in the north of my courtyard.

The BJP is becoming extremely strident and they have set three mosques on fire in Jaipur in celebration of their candidate's victory over the Congress candidate, Maharaja Bhawani Singh. Natwar Singh has been defeated in his new constituency of Mathura. The defeat of Devi Lal by our candidate, Mand, was very essential. For had he won, our claim to Abohar and Fazilka would have become very weak. The victory of Mand has settled that question once and for all. It's a signal for all outsiders that Punjab is shut for them. It's a historic verdict and Talwandi was very foolish in lending Akali support to Devi Lal. The new central leaders had put their eggs in Badal's basket and hoped they'd negotiate a settlement with him. The result in Punjab has upset many a politician's apple cart—the rout of Ramowalia, Jasowal, Calcutta,[34] and Shaminder Singh is a strong message that the panth will not brook such a species. It's also a message loud and clear to Devi Lal's friends that the Sikhs will run their politics from Amritsar and not Delhi. I should look up.

Today, I complete full five years of my imprisonment.

1 December 1989

I was sitting out in the sun when I saw a plane hover over my barrack over and over again. I thought the pilot was a novice and couldn't land for the plane looked like one from the BSF fleet. Later I was told that they were circling the jail to find my barrack and taking the watch tower as a landmark, and the clothes hung up for drying, they had spotted it.

[34] The name of a politician at the time.

The jailor came and sat with me. He's been good to me. He told me that Dilloo Bhenji had come and he escorted me to the office. She and Teddy Bhayaji were there. I broke down as I hugged her. She'd done the impossible—won me the elections handsomely—and now she was literally in charge, ordering the bureaucrats around, speaking to the governor and telling him what to do.

They didn't release me.

Sampat Singh, the Haryana home minister flew down. He'd gone to Amritsar and then come here. He said he'd come tomorrow with the orders for my release. It's this Vasudev Prasad, the prosecutor, who is playing up, and he's on record in the *Illustrated Weekly* as saying that even if the government withdrew the case he would go on and not allow it.

The sangat of Bhagalpur came and they brought me a langar.They gave me pershad, puris, and allu cholas.

I spoke to Geeta. She was cheerful. Dilloo Bhenji says she's a changed person. My children Emaan and Pavit spoke too. Little Nanki is in Chandigarh, ill as usual. Bibiji and Dads, Geeta and the two elder mites are in Amritsar awaiting my arrival. The mites wanted to know: 'When will you come, Papa?'

Dilloo Bhenji says that Pavit has been addressing huge election meetings and working very hard. All of them have moved heaven and earth to get me out of this cursed place. The Calcutta group[35] came too. Bhaiji Nirmal came and hugged me so tightly that I nearly collapsed. He's been a gem. Binay Babu came very sweetly with his band of Bengali lawyers. I paid him my deep respects. Poor man had to be lifted in a chair. He's too sweet. He came despite the fact that I had told Mr Mishra that I would personally come to call on him as soon as I was released. Dr Wadhera came, exhausted after a battle in court. He's told the prosecutor that he would not accept bail and only the withdrawal of the case would suit him. He looked so thrilled and was clad in a heavy Alaskan jacket.

At dusk the jailor asked me to retire to my ward. I bade everyone goodnight. V.P. Singh will take his oath tomorrow.Poor Jethmalani has been beaten black and blue by Chandrashekhar's men.

2 December 1989

I'm giving my odds and ends away. Dilloo Bhenji has come to take me home. I'll go now.

This diary, as I said, the last from jail, is for you my darling Dilloo Bhenji. I love you very very much. You have saved me from the scaffold and now we begin another adventure. The greatest in the service of the panth.

May God bless us and keep us from pride.

[35] This refers to the people who sheltered Papa when he was on the run in 1984.

I fear stepping out—for five years I have not seen the outside world.

While the votes were being counted I was back at school in Chandigarh after canvassing in Tarn Taran.

That was not where I wanted to be while everyone else was in Amritsar waiting for the election results to come in, but Mama wouldn't allow me to miss any more school.

Agatha Christie's *Ten Little Niggers*, performed at the PGI Auditorium, was YPS's annual play. The auditorium is packed. I sit next to Jasleen, my best friend. The curtains come down on the play and then they go up again—the headmaster is on the stage. We wonder if he'll announce a holiday. He clears his throat and says, 'There are two very lucky little girls here in the audience tonight, Pavit Kaur Mann and Nanki Kaur Mann—your father is coming home. Congratulations!'

A loud cheer goes up. Jasleen hugs me. After that is a big blank. I heard later that Nanki, sitting somewhere in the front, broke down and cried. I cannot remember how we went to Amritsar to receive Papa or any other details.

It's all gone. Even this incident comes to my mind because last night I was explaining to my twelve-year-old son why one cannot use the word 'nigger'. And there it was, this little flashback from twenty-four years ago.

It's strange how the human mind can close itself to painful memories, how they disappear into the recesses of the mind. I can sometimes remember a frock I wore when I was six years old, maybe even younger, with perfect clarity, and smile to myself at the crystal-clear memory of it.

Memories of Papa's imprisonment, however, get more and more vague and sometimes I begin to wonder if it was just a nightmare. But it did happen, and yes, it was a nightmare.

When I was in my last two years at boarding school in Sanawar, art was one of my subjects. My paintings were later analysed by a group of psychiatrists who visited us to study us as a family who had undergone the five years of Papa's imprisonment—they thought my paintings portrayed trauma.

I dismissed it as a lot of hogwash then but thinking back, painting may have been an outlet for my pain. There was no other way of expressing what one had gone through, for we, as Sikhs, are meant to stay strong.

I returned to Raja Sansi Airport in Amritsar where the family was waiting to finally receive my father, along with a huge excited crowd. The plane was due to arrive any minute. The waiting was almost too much to bear. Finally, the overzealous crowd broke through the doors and police cordons and went charging onto the tarmac.

We, the family, followed blindly, the police having quite a time trying to keep the situation under control. We stood aside in a small group, and suddenly I shouted, 'Mama, look there's the plane!' I would read these seemingly inconsequential words in the newspaper the next day, public as our lives had become.

Before the doors of the plane were even open, people clambered up the steps. I saw my father emerge from the surge of people; he looked confused and tired. Then he was gone from my vision again. I screamed 'Papa!', desperately, waving my hands as we pushed our way through the hordes in vain. Finally, we just stood aside, letting the crowds be with him. He was home now and we would have him to ourselves soon and hopefully, this time forever.

Everyone has a story to tell, some tell theirs and some choose not to. This is my story and after years I choose to tell it and lay it to rest once and for all.

Pa and me in Manali just after his release in 1989

Parliamentary Elections, April 2014

Twenty-five years later, Papa is standing for elections again from the Khadoor Sahib parliamentary constituency, or Tarn Taran as it was called the last time he stood from here while still in prison, and won with a record margin.

A lot has changed since then. Twenty-five years ago, this border constituency faced a huge threat from militancy and police excesses—almost every home had gruesome stories of terror to tell, of young boys being taken away in the dead of the night and being killed by the police on some pretext or the other. Today, the people of

Amiji with Pa shortly after his release

Tarn Taran are losing their youth to drugs, which are freely available all over Punjab, especially the areas close to the Pakistan border. From one misery to the next, the people of Punjab are disillusioned and very fed up, to the point where one feels embarrassed going around asking people to vote. From the Land of Milk and Honey, as Punjab was once called, it has now become a land of drugs, bullets, and to top it all, poisoned ground water[36]. The *Times of India*, 1 June 2014 has an interesting article written by Mark Tully, who says, 'The Khalistan cause may come out of the closet if issues like drugs and unemployment are not addressed.' Operation Blue Star and its aftermath resulted in absolute turmoil in the Punjab, creating the ground for a separate Sikh state. Today, the Sikhs, at least, within Punjab do not want Khalistan, but pushed against the wall, as they are being once again, this time by drugs and unemployment, another time bomb seems to be ticking away again.

Nanki and I have been going around the towns and campaigning for Papa in the bazaars, doing, 'door to door' as it's called but literally 'shop to shop', since we were assigned the markets. The heat is terrible, and added to the discontent of the people, the whole process isn't very heartening. Every time one breathes a sigh of relief seeing the end of a street, three new gallis, narrow lanes, open up

[36] With pesticides etc.

in front of one so one just goes on and on, till one literally collapses, as I did, of heat stroke.

What amazed me was that many old-timers still remembered a little girl asking people to vote for her father and bring him back to her from prison. Most point to Nanki and ask me if it was her. 'No,' I replied, with tears rolling down my cheeks, the first time I was asked, 'it was me . . .'

One old man asks me, 'Do you remember how we all got your father out of prison? With so much love, we even went to the polling booths barefoot as we'd promised we would, do you remember?'

Of course I remembered—how could I ever forget what these people did for us.

Epilogue

The Rubaiyat

'Tis alla Chequer-board of Nights and Days
Where Destiny with Men for Pieces plays:
Hither and thither moves, and mates, and slays,
And one by one, back in the Closet lays.

The Moving Finger writes; and, having writ,
Moves on: nor all thy Piety nor Wit
Shall lure it back to cancel half a Line,
Nor all thy Tears wash out a Word of it.

—Omar Khayyam

Acknowledgements

I WOULD LIKE to thank Random House India for taking me on and waiting patiently for me to finish writing, the editors assigned to me, Chiki Sarkar, Meru, and finally Archana Shankar, who will surely breathe a sigh of relief once this book is done. Thank you, Archana. Also, I would like to thank Pavan Bhen for getting me going and, of course, Mama and Papa, Virji, Nanki and my boys for helping at each stage and believing in me.

A Note on the Type

LINUX LIBERTINE IS a digital typeface, which aims to create free and open alternatives to proprietary typefaces such as Times Roman. It is a proportional serif typeface inspired by nineteenth-century book type. It contains more than 2,000 glyphs and encompasses character sets such as the Greek alphabet, Cyrillic script, and Hebrew alphabet. It also offers several ligatures and includes special characters such as International Phonetic Alphabet, arrows, floral symbols, Roman numbers, text figures and small caps.